Personnel Practices
In Adult Parole Systems

Personnel Practices
In Adult Parole Systems

By

CHARLES L. NEWMAN

Professor and Head
Law Enforcement and Corrections Services
College of Human Development
The Pennsylvania State University
University Park, Pennsylvania

CHARLES C THOMAS • PUBLISHER
Springfield • Illinois • U.S.A.

153647

Published and Distributed Throughout the World by
CHARLES C THOMAS • PUBLISHER
BANNERSTONE HOUSE
301-327 East Lawrence Avenue, Springfield, Illinois, U.S.A.
NATCHEZ PLANTATION HOUSE
735 North Atlantic Boulevard, Fort Lauderdale, Florida, U.S.A.

With THOMAS BOOKS *careful attention is given to all details of
manufacturing and design. It is the Publisher's desire to present books
that are satisfactory as to their physical qualities and artistic possibilities
and appropriate for their particular use.* THOMAS BOOKS *will be true
to those laws of quality that assure a good name and good will.*

Printed in the United States of America
A-2

Preface

In THE EARLY YEARS when the world was young, the penal code was the code of Hammurabi: "An eye for an eye and a tooth for a tooth." In America a century and a half ago, one state after another, in the formation of its constitution, declared that its penal code should be founded upon the principle of reformation and not of vindictive justice. Some states were a century in learning what the founding fathers meant when they wrote this principle into our Constitution; and, in many states, it is not yet understood.

As we peruse the state of the art of corrections in the second third of the twentieth century, we find, as the President's Crime Commission has documented, that, for too many offenders, corrections does not correct. To a great extent, this failure of corrections can be attributed to a lack of resources. Equally critical, however, is the widespread ignorance concerning how to use the resources which are available.

Corrections in the United States continues to be fragmented both administratively and operationally. Moreover, unlike other parts of the criminal justice system, it is the part which has lowest public visibility and about which least is known.

Such fragmentation contributes to lack of coherency within the correctional process. It also encourages redundance in certain types of activity (as, for example, in the collection of social history data). More importantly, however, fragmentation contributes to the omission of critical responsibilities because of non-accountability to other segments of the total system (as, for example, the failure of pre-sentence investigations to include meaningful strategies for institutional treatment when a recommendation for commitment is made, or the failure to parole at the optimal point of institutional correction).

In the final analysis, the success or failure of the correctional mission resides in the availability of sufficient resources and capable personnel. It must be noted here that capable personnel are those who, qualified by educational preparation, endowed with intelligence, equipped with a personal philosophy of humanistic values, and guided by competent leadership and direction, fulfill the objective of social restoration of the offender.

It is the contention of this work that the personnel matrix within corrections is vital to the competence of the system to achieve defined objectives. Simply stated, the strength and effectiveness of parole systems are determined by the adequacy, quality, and organization of people who are hired to do the job. The conditions under which they are recruited, selected, hired, supervised, rewarded, and nurtured will all bear on their capacity to fulfill societal expectations of the system. Given the diverse criteria for each of the foregoing personnel practices within the various states, it is not a great surprise to find that the quality of performance varies widely.

The data for this study came from the cooperation of many agency administrators throughout the United States. Their willingness "to tell it like it is" is recognized as their hope for improvement. To accomplish desired goals, however, takes much more than rhetoric, though discussion is a necessary part of identifying problems and describing objectives. Hopefully, the findings presented here will assist agencies to move ahead on their course toward an efficient and effective correctional process.

Almost three decades ago, the late Paul W. Tappan stimulated in me an interest in correctional administration. The enigmas which he posed have continued to serve as a challenge for the search, and to him and to his memory I am greatly indebted.

In succeeding years, a long list of professional colleagues in the field agencies supplemented my academic education with the practical realities which were drawn from their own experiences, thereby increasing my understanding of correctional problems and processes. To them and to my colleagues at the Florida State University, the University of Louisville, and the Pennsylvania State University, I owe a continuing debt of gratitude.

I would also like to acknowledge the considerable assistance afforded me by Dr. Benjamin Frank of the Joint Commission on Correctional Manpower and Training, who made available to me many unpublished staff documents which were part of the Commission's recent national study.

I am also much indebted to Professor C. Ray Jeffery of New York University who read the manuscript and provided much positive guidance in the completion of this study. His helpfulness will ever be remembered.

Finally, to my wife, Della Scott Newman, I offer my thanks for her patience, confidence, encouragement, and labor in typing many times the drafts and final manuscript. I reserve for myself whatever faults may be found in logic or presentation.

CHARLES L. NEWMAN
University Park, Pennsylvania

CONTENTS

Personnel Practices
In Adult Parole Systems

Chapter I

Nature of the Study

THIS STUDY IS CONCERNED with the administration of criminal justice. Specifically, it relates to parole administration, that segment of the correctional process which has responsibility for the post-institutional control and supervision of offenders released to it by an appropriate governmental body, more generally a parole board or commission.

In relation to parole administration, this study addresses itself to one phase of the theory of administration, namely personnel administration. Gulik has described administration as the art of getting things done, with the accomplishment of defined objectives.[1]

To that end, this study explores the administrative processes related to the personnel who get the work of the agency done. No definition can be expected to describe fully any subject or concept. But for the purposes of this study, personnel administration means that aspect of management which is concerned with: (a) the employment of workers (in this instance, those persons identified as parole officers or agents, and the various supervisory classes in relation to the parole officer role); (b) the organization of workers into efficient, informed groups to carry out the purposes of the organization; and (c) the development and administration of policies affecting their wellbeing as workers.[2]

---

[1]Luther Gulik: Science, values, and public administration. In Donald C. Rowatt (Ed.): *Basic Issues in Public Administration*. New York, Macmillan, 1965, p. 3.

[2]Harry L. Case: *Personnel Policy in a Public Agency*. New York, Harper, 1955, p. 4.

Parole and the Correctional System

Parole services for the public offender occur as the final stage in the correctional process, preceded by institutional commitment and a period of incarceration.[3] In a larger sense, it represents the culmination of society's intervention in the life of an individual who, initially, was accused of violating the law; secondly, was tried and convicted and, in lieu of probation, committed to the correctional institutional apparatus for control and behavior modification, punishment or treatment; and finally, was returned to the community for reintegration.

Two notions emerge from the fact that parole is a part of a larger system: (a) It may or may not be administratively integrated into the total criminal justice system. (The likelihood is the latter; that is, parole administration tends to be separate from other elements of the criminal justice system.)[4] (b) Many of the administrative problems experienced in the parole field are common to the other elements of the criminal justice system; including law enforcement, probation, and institutions at the federal, state, county, and municipal levels.[5]

As the final stage in the correctional process, parole services are frequently blamed for the performance failures found along the way. This is not to suggest any inherent superiority of parole service over that of other agencies which are involved with the offender. But, to cite several specific examples: failure of the courts to make proper use of pre-sentence investigation and disposition to the probation services; the sometimes poorly admin-

---

[3]Charles L. Newman: *Sourcebook on Probation, Parole, and Pardons*, 3rd ed. Springfield, Thomas, 1970, p. xii.

[4]Cf., The President's Commission on Law Enforcement and the Administration of Justice: *Task Force Report: Corrections.* Washington, Government Printing Office, 1967, p. 5. "Corrections is fragmented administratively, with the Federal Government, all fifty states, the District of Columbia, Puerto Rico, most of the country's 3,047 counties, and all except the smallest cities having one or more correctional facilities . . . Responsibility for the administration of corrections is divided not only among levels of government but also within single jurisdictions."

[5]*Ibid.* In February, 1967, the President's Commission on Law Enforcement and the Administration of Justice issued its general report: *The Challenge of Crime in a Free Society*, Washington, Government Printing Office, 1967. That volume details the multiple problems confronting the criminal justice system, and details recommendations for their amelioration. *Task Force Report: Corrections, op. cit.*, devotes chapter nine to "manpower and training," but considers personnel administration only peripherally to the purposes of this study.

istered and staffed probation services, per se; the rigidity of determinate penal sentences which disregard human factors in behavioral modification; a self-contradictory correctional philosophy, which seeks to punish and "treat" concurrently; the failure of the community to decide how it wants the correctional establishment to function; and the continued hostility of some law enforcement officials to the "ex-con;" among others, have a direct bearing upon the ultimate effectiveness and efficiency of parole services.[6]

Parole is a method of selectively releasing offenders from institutions, under supervision in the community, whereby the community is afforded continuing protection while the offender is making his adjustment and renewing his contribution to society.[7] Internally, the effectiveness of parole is contingent upon three aspects: (a) the construction of a sound philosophy which bears up under the most acute scrutiny of contemporary correctional philosophy; (b) fair and impartial administration; and (c) the establishment, maintenance, and operation of a sound personnel policy.

Basically, the strength and effectiveness of parole systems are determined by the adequacy and quality and organization of the necessary staff. Sound organization guarantees as nearly as possible the assignment of individuals to posts in which they are interested and for which they are qualified, where maximum opportunity for personal and professional growth is provided, and chance for advancement is available. Good organization assures, moreover, fair and equitable policies with regard to salary, working conditions, sick leave and health protection, and retirement provisions.

Of equally high importance is the type of leadership exercised by administrative boards and officers. The essential element, in

---

[6]The items *efficiency* and *effectiveness* are used here in the sense that Etzioni defines them: "The actual *effectiveness* of a specific organization is determined by the degree to which it realizes its goals. The *efficiency* of an organization is measured by the amount of resources used to produce a unit of output. Output is usually closely related to, but not identical with, the organizational goals." Amitai Etzioni: *Modern Organizations.* Englewood Cliffs, N.J., Prentice-Hall, 1966, p. 8.

[7]Charles L. Newman, *op. cit.,* p. 332. The National Conference on Parole (1956) considered terminology and parole concepts, in addition to other aspects. The definition provided at that meeting suggested inclusion of the phrase, "subject to conditions specified by the paroling authority" in addition to the definition provided here. The National Conference on Parole: *Parole in Principle and Practice.* New York, National Probation and Parole Association, 1957, p. 65.

the final analysis, of a well-integrated parole system is the service that it renders to the community and its clientele. If the working climate of the parole agency is such that each employee senses the importance of the correctional mission, and strives "to do his best," but at the same time recognizes that his role is part of a professional team, then the objectives of parole are more likely to be met, despite the hazards which were enunciated earlier.

Underlying Considerations

This is not a study of isolated facts, nor an agglomeration of those facts. It has been designed to identify and evaluate existing personnel practices in the parole field with the basic intention of measuring those practices against standards of personnel management and administration which have come to be accepted in the public administration field. Further, it is intended to present a picture of current parole personnel policies and practices, which, it is hoped, will serve as a stimulus to the upgrading of those personnel procedures by individual agencies.

The conceptualization of this study has been developed with an awareness that parole agencies differ in size, in the administrative placement within the scheme of governmental organization, and the magnitude of the correctional problems they uniquely face.[8] Thus, no set of generalizations will be presented which will attempt to suggest an ideal administrative scheme. It is hoped, however, that the insights gained in this study will be of value to administrators in parole agencies in that they will have a yardstick against which they can measure their own practices in the light of other states' performances and against national standards for administrative organization of parole services.[9]

Statement of the Problem

The present stage in the professional development of the parole field can only be evaluated in the light of the impressive accomplishments of the correctional field in the past one-and-a-half cen-

---

[8]This study is limited to parole administration on state levels, the federal system, and the parole services administered by the central units of the insular possessions. Local parole systems, where they exist in the United States, have been excluded from this study.

[9]The standards which shall be used in this study are derived from my own conceptions; the 1956 National Conference on Parole, *op. cit.*; the personnel standards as de-

turies—all of which were necessary before the focus of treatment could be approached. It is noteworthy that up to the past century, death, mutilation, or banishment were frequently the price for law violation.

The conception of an idea related to rehabilitation was in no small measure related to a number of basic changes in the social approach to the offender. Not the least among these included the following:

1. A doctrine of equality before the law.
2. The use of a penalty system in lieu of death.
3. A recognition of differentiations relating to age and mental competence in determining responsibility and disposition.
4. The provision of supervision in the community for selected offenders in lieu of institutionalization.
5. Classification of types of offenders and institutions.
6. A modification of institutional structure and program with the intent of reformation.[10]

With the change in orientation toward the offender came the concomitant change in societal relationship. The administration of the correctional idea necessitated the creation of a new body of personnel, organized into agencies.[11]

In parole, the improvement of the offender as a member of the

---

vised by the Professional Council of the National Council on Crime and Delinquency; and the reports developed for the Civil Service Assembly of the United States and Canada under the following titles: *Recruiting Applicants for the Public Service* (1942); *Placement and Probation in the Public Service* (1946); *Oral Tests in Public Personnel Selections* (1942); and *Employee Training in the Public Service* (1941). These reports constitute the most comprehensive set of criteria yet developed in personnel administration, though there is no dearth of text literature which restates the same general ideas. The work of the Joint Commission on Correctional Manpower and Training, currently in progress, will undoubtedly restate or codify many of the existing standards. "Standards for Selection of Probation and Parole Personnel" (Revised June, 1968, by an ad hoc committee of the Professional Council of NCCD, mimeo, 6 pp.), the American Correctional Association's *Manual of Correctional Standards* (1966).

[10]This typology was developed from a draft paper of the Council on Social Work Education, New York, made available to the author through the courtesy of Miss Mildred Sikkema.

[11]The movement in the direction of rehabilitation was substantially aided by the developments in the behavioral sciences and the associated helping professions. In many ways, the knowledge requisite to treatment of the offender predated the acceptance of such ideas by the field and community. Only in the past several decades has there been any demand for treatment that supports general investment of money, personnel, and organizational energy in the correctional process. *Ibid.*

social order is the expected result of the process of supervision and treatment. This improvement develops essentially, it is commonly believed, with the help of services of staff personnel of the parole agency. Since the human personalities of the parole officer, his supervisor, and administrator, are major factors in these services, the personnel area of parole administration assumes unusual significance.

Problem to be Examined

The problem of this study, then, is one of personnel administration. It seeks to determine what personal qualities are sought in the staff who are designated to carry out the correctional mission. The problem is a functional one, rather than one of basic research design, because it is geared to the ultimate improvement of parole services in the United States. The main problem is to determine how these parole personnel are recruited, examined, selected, oriented, evaluated, retained, or dismissed; how they are compensated, promoted, and encouraged to self-improvement. The problem is an important one, because without this knowledge we cannot know how close we are to uniform standards of personnel practice in adult parole systems in the United States. Moreover, with the increasingly free interchange of parolees under the Interstate Compact on Probation and Parole, it is vital to know that uniformly high quality of staff exists in every jurisdiction, not only for the benefit of the parolee and the protection of the community, but for the faith and confidence which should prevail between systems in the correctional field.[12]

In the past several decades, much has been written for and about the correctional field. Publications such as *Federal Proba-*

---

[12]In a report of the Attorney General of the United States, we find: "The subject of parole is vital in the administration of the criminal law. Interest in the matter is Nationwide, for maladministration of parole in one state is not limited in its effects to such state, but affects neighboring and sometimes even distant commonwealths. The principle of parole meets with the approbation of all enlightened and progressive criminologists and penologists. It is generally recognized that as a mode of transition for the prisoner from confinement in an institution to complete freedom, parole must form an important and vital part of the enforcement of the criminal law. On the other hand, it is likewise generally conceded that in many states, the administration of parole is frequently unscientific, lax, and inefficient...." Frank Murphy: *Annual Report of the Attorney General of the United States, 1939.* Washington, Government Printing Office, 1939, pp. 9-10. While the President's Crime Commission is not so direct in its statement, the report does indicate that "there are wide variations in practice" among jurisdictions. *Task Force Report: Corrections, op. cit.,* p. 67, *et seq.*

tion,[13] the *American Journal of Correction,[14] Crime and Delinquency,* the *Journal of Research in Crime and Delinquency,[15] Proceedings of the American Congress on Corrections,[16]* and *Yearbook* of the National Probation and Parole Association,[17] to mention a representative group, have been filled with ideas about, descriptions of, suggestions for, critiques of, and a miscellaneous *potpourri* regarding police, courts, probation, prisons, parole, delinquency, crime, social services, psychogenic factors, research methods, causes and cures of the correctional problem. *The Journal of Criminal Law, Criminology, and Police Science* has, in its criminology section, tended to limit itself to an academic consideration of the field. This has likewise been true of *Criminologica,* the journal of the American Society of Criminology.

However, in the vast amount of material which has been written, the sum total of which, by bibliographic reference, could fill many pages, the area of personnel administration in parole has been significantly lacking. The reasons for the void may be subject to conjecture.[18]

---

[13]Published by the Administration Office of the United States Courts, *Federal Probation* is a quarterly publication.

[14]The official publication of the American Correctional Association, this journal considers material mainly in the prison field. Now in its twentieth volume, it is successor to *Prison World,* which was retitled when the American Prison Association took on a correctional bent. Only minimal coverage is given to the parole field.

[15]The National Council on Crime and Delinquency, formerly the National Probation and Parole Association, is the professional association for the field of probation and parole. It represents the merger of the American Parole Association and the National Probation Association. The present journals are the newest format of the Association publications. Prior publications include *Focus* and *Probation* (discontinued January, 1959.)

[16]Published annually, these volumes contain papers presented by persons representing various organizations which comprise the Congress on Corrections. Topics range from culinary management in prisons to street club workers in delinquency areas. Parole administration and practices have received a fair share of consideration in these proceedings.

[17]The *Yearbook,* now discontinued, contained a collection of papers presented at the annual meeting of the Association. Almost no consideration was given to parole administration, per se, although much space was devoted to the desirability of developing sound correctional practices, of which parole is a part.

[18]It must be pointed out that the need for training and trained staff, as well as the need for adequate salaries, has received considerable attention. However, such other vital areas as recruitment, methods of selection, staff development organization, career service plans, retirement plans, etc., have received little attention. It may be significant to note that a similar void exists in the social work literature, where there has been far more concern with the dynamics of personality than with the organizational and administrative aspects of services.

On the other hand, the area of public administration has a plethora of material related to personnel administration and practices. Unfortunately, no attention has been paid to the area of parole administration, and as a consequence, this study represents the first effort to bring about an application of personnel administration theory to the parole field.[19]

Biases of the Study

Too frequently the area of administration is considered the direction of "things" in contrast to the more sound idea that it is the development of people. This study has assumed that the core of the correctional task influences every decision and action of administration and staff. Since the agency relationship with its clientele goes far beyond a formal structural design in the effort to modify and change behavior, it holds that matters of human relationships among personnel cannot be separated from the major function of task organization and the fulfillment of the goal of corrections.

The development of a quality corps of personnel requires planning, and it must be recognized that parole agencies are not only in competition with each other and companion correctional services, but also with private and public social services and private industry for the small supply of professionally trained individuals who seek entrance each year into the field. Thus, it is posited that every available device should be used by the parole agency to recruit the most qualified people from wherever they are available, without geographical, political, racial, or other distinction. One of the hypotheses of this study is that jurisdictions limit their recruitment potential because of the restrictiveness of their recruitment practices.

Once a pool of prospective employees becomes known to the agency, the task then is to select those individuals who have the training, skill, and personality to "fit" into the parole agency's

---

[19]The attempt to develop materials of personnel administration within a particular field of practice has had its proponents. Harold E. Moore and Newell B. Walters: *Personnel Administration in Education,* New York, Harper and Brothers, 1955; Herman Finer: *Administration and the Nursing Services,* New York, Macmillan, 1957; John J. Corson: *Executives for the Federal Service,* New York, Columbia, 1952; Alice C. Klein: *Civil Service in Public Welfare,* New York, Russell Sage, 1940.

function. This suggests that sound selection processes must operate, and that, hopefully, a high degree of uniformity should prevail between the parallel agencies in the various states.

Since there is no counterpart to parole work in civilian life or private industry, parole administrators must train all employees not only in the formal procedural elements involved in the parole process, but also the multitudinous duties related to the basic functions of parole supervision. Staff in-service training and development are considered here as vital components in the success of the correctional mission, and to the extent to which these programs operate, give a clue, at least, to the efforts of the agency to improve the quality of service it is offering to its clientele and ultimately to the public.

It is further assumed that beyond the point of recruitment and selection, appointment, and training, agencies must develop techniques which allow for the periodic evaluation of staff. Such ratings not only assure the agency that the staff person is functioning according to acceptable standards, but also provide a means whereby the worker is given some clue as to the adequacy of his performance, areas needing improvement, and the recognition of special talent. Moreover, since it is assumed that the agency will need a continuing supply of supervisory and administrative staff, the evaluation of past performance of staff members would give some clue as to the potentially most desirable candidates.

In the long range planning for corrections, conditions of employment take on special relevance. It is essential that the salaries of correctional personnel be maintained in an equitable relation to the cost of living and to the salaries of other positions carrying comparable responsibilities and requirements. While the scope of this study does not include a comparative analysis of salaries between fields, it can be shown that salaries in the parole field vary significantly between states; that, on the whole, salaries tend to be lower in the parole field than in other areas of the social welfare field. Further, it shall be demonstrated that such salary conditions have tended to act as a barrier to effective recruitment and retention of qualified staff.

Other conditions, such as the nature of employment on a career or political appointment basis, will undoubtedly affect the quality of performance found within the agency. The security of tenure, achieved after a rigorous probationary period, affords the employees the comfort of knowing that a change of administration will not alter the permanency of their positions and that the effectiveness of their performance will be the sole guide to any action involving separation.

Moreover, the awarding of such tenure tends to assure that a careful screening process will first be invoked and that the incompetents will be eliminated in the selection process. Not only will the agency be assured of a higher quality staff, but the public will have the opportunity to gain more confidence in the staffing of the public service. The benefits which evolve from such public confidence cannot be questioned.

Our culture has long reflected the desirability of rewarding long periods of faithful and effective service with retirement pay. The correctional employee, the very nature of whose job reflects the protection of society, should be entitled to the same benefits granted to employees of other public and private services and industry. This study has attempted to determine to what degree these benefits currently exist.

Sources of Data

The inputs of data for this study have been derived from a number of sources. An intensive search of the literature in the field of correctional administration was made in order to isolate all previous studies, reports, manuals, and other data related to personnel administration in the field of parole.[20] The unpublished data of the Joint Commission on Correctional Manpower and Training provided a major source of current statistical information.[21]

---

[20]A major finding of this documentary analysis has been that no study equal either in intensity or magnitude has ever been made in the United States related to parole personnel administration.

[21]With the passage of the Correctional Rehabilitation Study Act in September, 1965, a three-year study of correctional manpower practices and needs was authorized. The Joint Commission on Correctional Manpower and Training, funded by this act, has the responsibility to produce a detailed appraisal of needs and specific proposals for meeting them. The Commission staff is now engaged in conducting these extensive studies. For the circumstances leading to the development of the Manpower Commission and the successor legislation, see Charles S. Prigmore (Ed.): *Manpower and Training for Corrections: Proceedings of an Arden House Conference, June 24-26, 1964*. New York, Council on Social Work Education, 1966.

Through the courtesy and cooperation of the National Council on Crime and Delinquency, various confidential field reports were made available for examination and study. Some of these reports are identified in the text. Others are not so designated because of their nature. The report of the National Conference on Parole,[22] the standards of the American Correctional Association,[23] and the recommendations contained therein, became the major framework against which the findings were evaluated.

Parole services are usually organized as a bureau or department under the direction of a state paroling authority.[24] Thus, the individual state parole agencies became the major sources of data regarding personnel policies and practices. In view of this, two separate communications were sent to each of the fifty states,[25] insular possessions,[26] the federal system,[27] and the District of Columbia.[28] The first communication directed a request for job descriptions of all administrative, supervisory, and field personnel in the parole agency. Since this study is concerned primarily with the functional aspects of personnel administration to agency services, clerical and other nonprofessional services were excluded from this study. A second communication was later directed to the same agencies which included an extensive questionnaire covering the major areas of concern in this study: recruitment, selection, staff training, compensation and career service plans, and administrative organization.[29] Responses were received from forty jurisdictions, as indicated in Appendix A.

Finally, interviews with various members of the staff of the American Correctional Association, the National Council on Crime

---

[22]National Probation and Parole Association: *Parole in Principle and Practice, op. cit.* (Report of a conference called by the Attorney General of the United States.) At this conference, a series of standards were prepared and accepted by 475 representatives of the parole field.

[23]American Correctional Association: *Manual of Correctional Standards,* 3rd ed. Washington, The Association, 1966.

[24]See Chapter II.

[25]To the department or agency responsible for the administration of parole services.

[26]Puerto Rico, Virgin Islands.

[27]The Administrative Office of the United States Courts, and the United States Board of Parole, and the District of Columbia.

[28]Virgin Islands and Puerto Rico were later excluded for lack of response to inquiries.

[29]See Appendix C for questionnaire.

and Delinquency, the Joint Commission on Correctional Manpower and Training, parole agency administrators, and the Council on Social Work Education uncovered anecdotal information and sources of unpublished material which provided references which are reflected throughout this study.

The material in the subsequent chapters reflects the findings of this study. The initial hypothesis which cited the lack of uniform personnel policies and practices in parole administration has, on the whole, been substantiated. In general, availability of personnel has not been indicated as a problem, primarily because criteria for qualifications have been considerably lower in most states than the standards suggest.[30] Contrary to a corollary hypothesis, staff turnover, for two years at least, has been relatively low. Inadequate salary levels and lack of promotional opportunities are problems in most jurisdictions. Moreover, the development of staff potentialities to their maximum appears to be delegated to a secondary role in the light of staff shortages and excessive caseloads.

---

[30]Chapter IV, *infra.*, The National Survey on Corrections, whose findings are reported by the President's Crime Commission, found that in 1965, 41 percent of the adult parole agencies either lacked educational requirements (21 percent) for employment, or required only high school graduation (20 percent). No agency required a graduate degree. *Task Force Report: Corrections, op cit.*, p. 94.

Chapter II

The Nature of Organization
For Correctional Service

IN THE PREVIOUS CHAPTER, parole was defined as a status sometimes granted to an incarcerated offender, based upon an administrative decision that he could, with supervision, live in the community without reestablishing his pattern of criminal activity. Now,
from a somewhat different frame of reference, parole is to be
considered as a governmentally-administered service, requiring leg-
islative enactment, administrative management and decision making, judicial or quasi-judicial selection and revocation processes,
an organized personnel, policies, and procedures. We begin with
an analysis of the emergence of the current organizational scheme.

Organizational Scheme

American correctional services vary widely in the nature of their
formal organization. They differ in the size of their operation,
the numbers and professional preparation of their staffs, the quality
of service they render, the philosophy of their chief administrator,
their ultimate goals, and their place in the organizational scheme
of the state government. The diversity should not be regarded as
the inability of certain individuals to see things "right". Rather,
the variations exist because of historical accident, differential value
systems, and a host of other factors, not least among which was
the task of fitting newly emerging correctional organizations into
existing governmental structures.

The variation in structural organization of the various parole
systems in the United States is found in Table I.

TABLE I

ORGANIZATION OF PAROLE SYSTEMS IN U.S.: STRUCTURE[1]

State	Structure
Alabama	The Alabama State Board of Pardons and Paroles is an independent State agency. The Chief of Field Parole Services is administratively responsible to the Board. The Board consists of three full-time members, appointed by the Governor for staggered six-year terms.
Alaska	All correctional services have been integrated into a single administrative unit—the Youth and Adult Authority, a division of the Alaska Department of Health and Welfare. The Board of Parole is placed in the Authority. The Board Chairman is Director of the Authority. Two other members serve four-year terms.
Arizona	The Arizona Board of Pardons and Paroles is an independent State agency. The Chairman of the Board is Supervisor of parolees. The other two Board members are elected public officials serving as ex-officio, (Attorney-General and Superintendent of Public Instruction). They choose the third member who serves as Chairman.
Arkansas	The Board of Pardons, Paroles, and Probation is an independent State agency. The State Director of the Division of Probation and Parole Services is responsible to the Board. The membership of the Board consists of five part-time, honorary members appointed by the Governor for five-year terms. The Chairman is elected from the Board membership, after the Governor has designated his preference.
California	The Adult Authority is a part of the State's Youth and Adult Corrections Agency, and has responsibility for male offenders. The Board of Trustees-California Institution for Women is also a part of the Youth and Adult Corrections Agency. The Board consists of five part-time members appointed by the Governor for staggered four-year terms. The Adult Authority consists of seven full-time members appointed by the Governor for staggered four-year terms. Field services for men and women are provided by the Parole and Community Services Division of the Department of Corrections.
Colorado	The Colorado Board of Parole is an independent agency within the governmental structure of the State. It is the paroling authority; however, the Department of Parole, which provides field supervision, is administratively within the State Department of Institutions. The Board consists of seven part-time members, five of whom are appointed for six-year terms. Two members are ex-officio constitutional members, namely the Governor and Attorney-General.
Connecticut	The Board of Parole in Connecticut is an independent State agency. Its membership consists of three part-time, unpaid members. The Division of Parole in the Department of Corrections administers field

[1]The basic data for this table is derived from the compilation, National Parole Institutes: *A Survey of the Organization of Parole Systems.* New York, National Council on Crime and Delinquency, 1963, Publication III, 133 pp. Material was updated from the 1968 edition of the *Directory of Correctional Institutions and Agencies of U.S.A., Canada, and Great Britain.* Washington, The American Correctional Association, July, 1968. Additional data was derived from private conversations with various professional staff of the National Council on Crime and Delinquency. See also, Garrett Heyns: Patterns of Correction. *Crime and Delinquency,* XIII: 421-431, July, 1967.

State	Structure

parole services. A different Parole Board, serving four-year terms and consisting of seven part-time members, grants parole from the Connecticut Reformatory. Parole field services are directly administered by the Superintendent of the Reformatory. Female offenders are considered for parole by a Board of Directors of the Connecticut State Farm and Prison for Women. That Board, consisting of seven part-time members, serves seven-year terms, with one member's term expiring each year.

Delaware   The Delaware Board of Parole is an independent agency within the State governmental structure. The Board consists of three part-time members appointed by the State Supreme Court for three-year terms. Though the State has a Department of Corrections, the Parole Commission, which provides field supervision, is not part of it.

District of Columbia   The Board of Parole is an independent agency within the governmental structure of the District of Columbia. The Board consists of one full-time and four part-time members. The full-time member is designated as Parole Executive. Membership on the Board is for three years, at the pleasure of the D.C Board of Commissioners. Field services are administered by the Division of Parole Supervision in the Department of Corrections.

Florida   The Florida Probation and Parole Commission is an independent State agency. Three full-time members serve staggered six-year terms. An Administrative Assistant is responsible for the administration of the field services for adult parole and probation services.

Georgia   The State Board of Pardons and Paroles in Georgia is an independent agency. It consists of three full-time members, appointed by the Governor for staggered seven-year terms. The Chief of Field Parole Services is administratively responsible to the Board.

Hawaii   The Board of Paroles and Pardons functions within the framework of the State Department of Social Services.[2] The Board is composed of five part-time, nonsalaried members, appointed by the Governor for four-year terms. The field parole services are responsible to the Board's Executive Secretary.

Idaho   The Idaho State Board of Corrections is an independent State agency, and acts in a triple capacity: (1) as the Board of Corrections, it considers administrative parole and probation matters; (2) as the Board of Pardons, it considers pardons, commutations, and remissions; (3) executive functions, including the administration of the state penitentiary, rehabilitation, and probation and parole services. The Board consists of three full-time members, appointed by the Governor for staggered six-year terms. The Secretary of the Board serves as Director of Probation and Parole Services.

Illinois   The Parole and Pardon Board in Illinois is a division of the Department of Public Safety. The Board consists of seven part-time members, appointed by the Governor for staggered four-year terms. The Chief of the Division of Supervision of Parolees is administratively responsible to the Board.

---

[2]However, the quasi-judicial functions of the Board of Paroles and Pardons are not subject to approval, review, or control of the head of the Department of Social Services. National Parole Institutes, Publication III, *op. cit.,* p. 33.

State	*Structure*
Indiana	The Indiana Parole Board is a division of the Department of Corrections. The Board consists of three full-time members who serve staggered four-year terms. Board members are recommended by the Commissioner of Corrections and approved by the Governor. The Division of Parole in the Department of Correction is administratively responsible for the field parole services.
Iowa	The Board of Parole is an independent agency within the governmental structure of the State of Iowa. The Board consists of three part-time members, appointed by the Governor to six-year terms, staggered every two years. Field services are provided by the Bureau of Adult Correction Services in the Department of Social Services.
Kansas	The Kansas Board of Probation and Parole is an independent State agency which has administrative jurisdiction over the field parole functions. The Board consists of three full-time members, appointed by the Governor to four-year overlapping terms.
Kentucky	The Kentucky Parole Board is attached to the Department of Corrections for administrative purposes. The Board is composed of five full-time members who serve four-year terms. They are appointed by the Governor from a list from the Commission on Correction and Community Service. The Department of Corrections provides personnel to assist the Board as is necessary. Administrative responsibility over field parole and probation services is vested within the Department, as is the Director of the Division of Probation and Parole.
Louisiana	The Louisiana Board of Parole is within the Department of Institutions for administrative purposes.[3] The Governor appoints five part-time members whose terms run concurrently with his own. Field services are provided by the Division of Probation and Parole in the Department of Corrections.
Maine	In Maine, the Probation and Parole Board is part of the Department of Mental Health and Corrections.[4] In terms of its quasi-judicial function, the Board acts as an independent agency. The Board is composed of three part-time members, one of whom is the Commissioner of the Department of Mental Health and Corrections, whose term is three years. The other two part-time members serve terms of four years, appointed by the Governor. The Director of the Division of Probation and Parole is administratively responsible to the Department of Mental Health and Corrections.
Maryland	The Board in the State of Maryland is part of the Department of Parole and Probation. The Board is appointed by the Governor and is composed of three members who serve staggered six-year terms.[5] The Chairman of the Board is also the Director of the Department of Parole and Probation. The Chief of field parole services is administratively responsible to the Director of the Department.

---

[3]The Board is autonomous in regard to its policies and decisions relative to the parole of prisoners.

[4]For the purpose of accounting and the fixing of fiscal responsibility.

[5]The Chairman is a full-time member; two are part-time associate members.

State	*Structure*

Massachusetts   The Parole Board is an agency within the Department of Corrections, but not subject to its jurisdiction, and acts as an independent State entity. The Board consists of five full-time members who serve staggered five-year terms. All members are appointed by the Governor. The Director of Parole Services is administratively responsible to the Parole Board.

Michigan   The Michigan Parole Board is an agency within the State Department of Corrections. The Board consists of five full-time civil service employees who serve indefinite terms.[6] All field staff services are provided by the Bureau of Field Services of the Department of Corrections.

Minnesota   The Minnesota Adult Corrections Commission is an agency within the Department of Corrections.[7] The Commission is comprised of a full-time Chairman, who is appointed by the Commissioner of Corrections, and four other members who are appointed by the Governor for terms of six years on a staggered basis. The Chairman serves at the pleasure of the Commissioner of Corrrections. The Chief of field parole services is administratively responsible to the Chairman of the Commission in his role as Deputy Commissioner of the Division of Adult Corrections.

Mississippi   The Mississippi Probation and Parole Board is an independent State agency with jurisdiction over field probation and parole services. The Board is composed of four full-time members, appointed by the Governor, for four-year terms. The Board's Executive Officer administers field services.

Missouri   The Board of Probation and Parole is a Division within the Department of Corrections with direct responsibility to the Governor. The Board consists of three full-time members who serve staggered six-year terms. All members are appointed by the Governor. The Chief Field Supervisor is responsible to the Board for the administration of field services.

Montana   The Montana Board of Pardons is an independent State agency with administrative jurisdiction over field parole functions. The Board consists of three part-time members, appointed by the Governor for staggered six-year terms. The Director of field services is administratively responsible to the Board.

Nebraska   The Board of Probation and parole is a Division within the Departmental structure of the State of Nebraska. The Board is composed of three ex-officio members as provided by the State Constitution.[8] The Chief of field services is administratively responsible to the Board of Pardons.

---

[6] Board members are appointed by the Corrections Commission and are removable only for cause.

[7] The Chairman of the Adult Corrections Commission functions as the Deputy Commissioner of the Division of Adult Corrections, which has the responsibility for adult field services and the administration of adult correctional institutions.

[8] These members are, by virtue of their office, the Governor, Secretary of State, and Attorney General. The term of office of Board members is determined by the term of office in their respective elective positions. By the nature of their other offices, Board members are necessarily part-time.

State	*Structure*
Nevada	The Nevada Department of Parole and Probation is an independent State agency. The Board consists of five full-time members, appointed by the Governor to four-year overlapping terms. The Chief Parole and Probation Officer is responsible to the Board for field parole services.
New Hampshire	The Board of Parole is an independent State agency. The Board consists of seven part-time members, six of whom are appointed by the Governor, and serve for staggered six-year terms. A seventh member is on the Governor's Council and is assigned to serve on the Board of Parole for a two-year term, which is his tenure as a Councilor. The Board appoints a State Parole Officer to serve as Administrative Officer and Chief of Parole Services.
New Jersey	The New Jersey State Parole Board is within the framework of the Department of Institutions and Agencies. The Board is composed of three members. The Chairman is full-time and the associate members are part-time. Board members are appointed by the Governor for a term of six years. The Chief of field parole services is administratively responsible to the Director of the Division of Corrections and Parole within the Department of Institutions and Agencies.
New Mexico	The Board of Probation and Parole is an independent agency within the governmental structure of the State of New Mexico. The Board consists of five part-time members, appointed by the Governor, who serve six-year staggered terms. Field services are provided by the Adult Probation-Parole Division of the Department of Corrections.
New York	The Board of Parole is an independent State agency. The Board consists of nine full-time members who serve staggered six-year terms. All are appointed by the Governor. The Chairman functions as the Chief administrative officer of the Division of Parole in the Executive Department.
North Carolina	The Board of Paroles is an independent State agency. The Board is appointed by the Governor and consists of three full-time members who serve staggered four-year terms. It appoints a Chief Parole Officer who is responsible for the administration of the Board's field services.
North Dakota	The North Dakota State Board of Pardons and Paroles is an independent agency within the governmental structure of the state. The Board is made up of five part-time members, three of whom are ex-officio.[9] Two citizen members are appointed by the Governor for a term of two years. The Board has administrative responsibility over the field parole function.
Ohio	The Pardon and Parole Commission is a unit of the Department of Mental Hygiene and Corrections for administrative purposes. The Commission consists of five full-time members, appointed by the Governor, for staggered six-year terms. The Adult Parole Authority of the Department of Mental Hygiene and Corrections provides field services.

---

[9]The three ex-officio, constitutional members are the Governor, the Attorney-General, and Chief Justice of the Supreme Court. The constitution designates the Governor as Chairman of the Board.

State	Structure
Oklahoma	The Board of Pardon and Parole is an independent State agency. The Board consists of five part-time members, three of whom are appointed by the Governor, one by the Chief Justice of the Supreme Court, and one by the presiding judge of the Court of Criminal Appeals. The Division of Probation and Parole in the Department of Corrections is in charge of field services.
Oregon	The Oregon Board of Parole and Probation is an independent State agency. The Board consists of five part-time members appointed by the Governor to five-year terms. Administrative jurisdiction over field parole is provided by the Probation and Parole Section of the Corrections Division.
Pennsylvania	The Board of Probation and Parole is an independent State agency. The Board consists of five full-term members appointed by the Governor to serve four-year terms. The Board appoints a Superintendent of Parole Services, who is responsible for the administration of the Board's field services.
Rhode Island	The Rhode Island Parole Board operates within the framework of the Department of Social Welfare for administrative purposes. The Board is composed of three part-time members appointed by the Governor for a staggered three-year term.[10] The Board has a full-time Executive Secretary to assist it in the administration of its function. The administrator of the Probation and Parole Department is responsible to the Department of Social Welfare, and for field services.
South Carolina	The South Carolina Probation, Parole, and Pardon Board is an independent State agency. The Board consists of six part-time members appointed by the Governor for terms of twelve years on a staggered basis, one term expiring every two years. The Director of the State Department of Probation and Parole is administratively responsible to the Board.
South Dakota	South Dakota Board of Pardons and Paroles is an independent State agency. The Board consists of three part-time members.[11] Two Board members serve a four-year term. The Director of the State Department of Probation and Parole is administratively responsible to the Board.
Tennessee	The Tennessee Board of Pardons, Paroles, and Probation is within the State Department of Corrections. The Board consists of five members. One of these is full-time and is the Commissioner of Corrections. The four part-time members and the Commissioner serve at the pleasure of the Governor. The Director of the Division of Probation and Parole is the Chief of field services and is responsible to the Board.

---

[10]The Rhode Island statutes set forth qualifications for appointment to the Parole Board as follows: one to be a physician, professionally qualified in the field of psychiatry or neurology; one to be a member of the Rhode Island Bar in good standing; and one who is professionally trained in the field of corrections or some related field of social work.

[11]One member is an Assistant Attorney General who serves for the duration of the term of the Attorney General appointing him. The second member is appointed by the Governor, and the third by the South Dakota Supreme Court.

State	Structure
Texas	The Board of Pardons and Paroles is an independent State agency. The Board consists of three full-time members who serve staggered six-year terms. One member is appointed by the Governor, one by the Chief Justice of the Supreme Court, and one member by the presiding judge of the Court of Criminal Appeals.[12] The Board appoints a Director of the Division of Parole Supervision, who is Chief of Field Services.
U.S. Board of Parole	The Board consists of eight full-time members appointed by the President for staggered six-year terms. The Board has no field services of its own, and the U.S. Probation Officers act as parole agents for the Board.[13]
Utah	The Board of Pardons is a Division of the Utah State Board of Corrections. The Board consists of three part-time members appointed by the Board of Corrections to serve for a term of six years.[14] Administration of the Board of Pardons and the Department of Adult Probation and Parole is vested in the Board of Corrections. The Chief Agent of the Adult Probation and Parole Section, Division of Corrections, is administratively responsible to the Department of Social Services.
Vermont	The Governor's Advisory Parole Board functions within the framework of the Department of Institutions.[15] The Advisory Parole Board is composed of three part-time members appointed by the Governor for staggered six-year terms. The Board appoints the Commissioner of Institutions (with the approval of the Governor), and the Director of Parole and Probation Services is administratively responsible to the Commissioner.
Virginia	The Virginia Parole Board is an agency within the Department of Welfare and Institutions. The relationship between the Board and the Department is primarily that of a service relationship. The Board consists of three full-time members appointed by the Governor for staggered six-year terms. The Board administers the field parole services through its Executive Secretary.[16]
Washington	The Board of Prison Terms and Paroles is an independent State agency. The Board consists of five full-time members who serve staggered five-year terms. All are appointed by the Governor. The Board of Institutions appoints a Chief Probation and Parole Officer, who is responsible for field services through the Division of Probation and Parole.
West Virginia	The West Virginia Board of Probation and Parole is an independent State agency. The Board consists of three full-time members appointed by the Governor for six-year terms. The Board is organized into three Divisions, each the responsibility of one of the members. The Board exercises administrative jurisdiction over field functions.

[12]All appointments are subject to the approval of the State Senate.

[13]U.S. Probation Officers are appointed by Federal District Courts.

[14]The terms are staggered so that every two years there is a vacancy which the Board of Corrections must fill.

[15]In addition to its advisory parole function to the Governor, it also sits as a Board of Institutions for state hospitals, prisons, reform schools, and sanitoriums.

[16]Parole Officers are appointed by the Circuit Court Judges, in the areas included in the parole districts, from eligible lists submitted by the Parole Board.

State	Structure
Wisconsin	The Parole Board is a part of the staff of the Director of the Department of Health and Social Services. The Director of the Division of Correction of the Department of Public Welfare is Chairman of the Board. The Board consists of five members in addition to the Chairman. All are full-time civil service appointees.[17] Field services are provided by the Bureau of Probation and Parole.
Wyoming	The Wyoming Board of Pardons is an independent State agency. The Board is composed of five elected State officials: the Governor, the Secretary of State, the State Auditor, the State Treasurer, and the State Superintendent of Public Instruction.[18] The operation of field services is vested in the State Probation and Parole Officer, who is responsible to the Board.
Puerto Rico	The Governor of the Commonwealth of Puerto Rico may grant pardons and reprieves and remit fines and forfeitures for offenses committed against the laws of Puerto Rico. Parole supervision is by parole officers of the Board.
Virgin Islands	The Parole Board is in the Department of Public Safety.[19]
District of Columbia	The Board of Parole for the District of Columbia does not have a field staff. Its cases are supervised for it by the District of Columbia Department of Corrections through its Division of Parole Supervision.

From the foregoing data, we have seen that there are diverse schemes for fitting correctional services in the overall structure of state government.

The National Survey of Corrections found that the institutions in forty-seven jurisdictions operate under some type of central agency.[20] In some states, institutions are placed under a department of welfare; in others, under a board of institutions. A department of corrections is the most common arrangement for institutional placement. However, these departments vary greatly in the extent to which they have reduced the administrative autonomy of the individual correctional institutions. In only a few instances

---

[17]Persons who are appointed have life-time tenure, subject to the usual civil service regulations. Civil service requirements for Board membership generally include two years of graduate training in an accredited school of social work or related discipline and eight years of progressively responsible experience in a corrections program.

[18]Membership on the Board runs concurrent with the tenure of their elective office. In addition to serving on the Board of Pardons, members also sit on twenty other Boards and Commissions.

[19]No other information available. The 1966 *Annual Report* of the Government of the Virgin Islands of the United States indicated a total budgetary expenditure for the Parole Board of $174. Department of Public Safety: *1966 Annual Report: July 1, 1965—June 30, 1966*, Charlotte Amalie.

[20]President's Crime Commission; *Task Force Report: Corrections*, p. 59.

is there a linkage of the total correctional administrative operation, including probation services, institutions, and parole supervision.[21]

In the adult parole field, with which we are concerned, the independent agency is the characteristic mode, inasmuch as forty-one states operate within that pattern. In seven states, the parole board is a unit within a larger department of state government. In two states, the parole board is the same body that regulates the correctional institutions. However, in the adult field, the final power to grant or deny parole is never given to the staff directly involved in the operation of a correctional institution.[22] In contrast, the juvenile field is quite different; where, in thirty-four out of fifty states, release decisions are made directly by the institutional operating staff.[23]

Historical Considerations

Elmer Johnson points out that decentralization marked the origin of correctional agencies.[24] Initially, states limited their correctional responsibilities to prisons. Because there was usually only one prison, the scope of activities and emphasis on localization of authority favored development of an autonomous board reporting directly to the Governor. In the late nineteenth and early twentieth centuries, it became the custom to have many state functions performed by commissions or boards. This was part of the general reform movement of the period—a reaction to the low standards of performance prevalent among some public officials in many jurisdictions.[25]

The impression, at the time, was that nonpartisan or bipartisan boards would check the influence of "politics" upon the conduct of public business. The problems of administration were not recognized, or if they were, it was assumed that several citizens, serving

---

[21]Garrett Heyns: Patterns of correction. *Crime and Delinquency, 13*: 421-433, July, 1967.

[22]President's Crime Commission, *op. cit.,* p. 65.

[23]*Ibid.,* p. 65. See also, Maurice A. Harmon: Unravelling Administrative Organization in State Juvenile Services. *Crime and Delinquency, XIII*: 436-437, July, 1967.

[24]Elmer H. Johnson: *Crime, Correction, and Society.* Homewood, Ill., Dorsey Press, 1968, pp. 536-537.

[25]Council of State Governments: *Reorganizing State Government.* Chicago, The Council, 1950, pp. 14-16.

as watchdogs on behalf of the public, would meet the need. Cleveland and Buck point out that with the rapid expansion of governmental activities at the turn of the century, as new agencies were established, it was natural that boards or commissions were set up to head them.[26]

By World War I, some defects began to be seen in areas of government with the use of lay or ex-officio boards and commissions. Essentially, the problems of government were becoming too complex to be handled by boards of lay officials. Then, too, as the prestige of the reform movements ebbed, citizens of prominence and ability tended to be replaced by strictly party appointees.

The Trend Toward Professionalization

Another development has been the rapid professionalization of public services.[27] The functions of state government have developed rapidly in areas where specialized knowledge and competence is essential and inevitable. In public education, public health, and public welfare—three of the great servant fields which require large portions of state budgets and staff—there have been tremendous developments in professionalism in this century. In law enforcement, probation and parole, and correctional institutions, there are notable developments in the requirements of special professional training.[28]

The key to understanding the many complex problems of the entire correctional field is to identify and take hold of what is essential among the many varied services performed by institutions, agencies, and officials. When that point is reached, it should be possible to emerge with sound programs. It is questionable, however, whether an untrained lay group has either the capacity or the depth of focus to see the problems of the correctional field in their proper perspective.

Another practice still too widespread in parole administration

[26]Fredrick A. Cleveland and A. S. Buck: *The Budget and Responsible Government.* New York, Macmillan, 1920, pp. 113-117.

[27]American Assembly: *The 48 States: Their Tasks as Policy Makers and Administrators.* New York, Columbia University, 1955, pp. 119-131.

[28]The trend toward professionalization is not limited to the U.S. See for example, John Conrad: *Crime and Its Correction: An international Survey of Attitudes and Practices.* Berkeley, University of California Press, 1965, Ch. 3.

is that of having its important functions performed by ex-officio boards. This practice is especially prevalent in states that elect several administrative officials. In addition to serving as department heads, these elected officers usually have a number of other board memberships. The most common argument in favor of ex-officio boards is one of economy. However, where a field such as corrections is dedicated to the responsibility for control, influence, and redirection of human beings, it is questionable whether economy can really be derived from such an arrangement, particularly when board members are so busy with their major functions that necessary time to devote to parole adjudication matters can often be lacking. Therefore, such boards either accomplish virtually nothing, or they must hire an executive director to serve as operating head.[29]

Parole Board Membership

Membership to the board of parole is generally made by the governor. In most states there are no statutory qualifications for appointment to the board. Generally such positions are not covered under a classification plan of the state personnel system. The period of appointment ranges from two to six years, with confirmation by one or both houses of the legislature sometimes required. There is an increasing trend among the states to require that a particular profession be represented on the board. Thus, to cite specific examples, California, Iowa, Rhode Island, and Tennessee statutes require that one member of the board be an attorney. A penologist must be on the board in California, Idaho, New Jersey, and Rhode Island. Other states require that membership on the parole board include such professions as sociologist, psychiatrist, physician, peace officer, neurologist, and persons trained in business administration. The basic justification for the body politic, a union of the people in the form of government, whether local, statewide, or national in scope, must be the protection of life and property of its members and the strengthening of the character of its individual and collective membership, through educational,

---

[29] It is a rather frightening thought that commitment to an institution can be made by one judge, but a panel of three or more parole board members must agree on release. Some means of modifying parole adjudication must be created.

welfare, and rehabilitative programs. To this end, the parole board has the responsibility for formulating programs of treatment and control geared to the individuality and need of both the community and the parolee entrusted to it for supervision. Hopefully, the parole board does not parole prisoners solely to reduce the penal population, meet a quota, or respond to an economic situation, inasmuch as such actions would always cost the taxpayers far more in repeated acts of crime, and at the same time deprive the law abiding citizens of the protection of life and property to which they are entitled.

Three major groups of problems are apparent in the operation and organization of parole boards. The first group pertains to the process of decision making: the securing of equitable, consistent, realistic decisions as to the length of time to be served by inmates before release. The second area deals with the board functions not directly concerned with the hearing of cases. In various ways the board must be concerned with general policy formation, public interpretation, administration, research and evaluation, and other administrative concerns. The third group of problems concerns the question of the best organization of the board for the accomplishment of the functions just noted.

In no small measure, the decision-making process in regard to the inmate is related to the entire penal-correctional philosophy of the culture in which the agency is found. A public which sees parole as a "frill," or a softness on the part of the correctional authorities, is bound to give little or no support to the parole mission. When a parole system is attached to a penal structure where the philosophical base is retributive rather than correctional, the parole board and its field agents are immeasurably handicapped in carrying out their mission. Hence, lacking uniformity in correctional processes among the states, we cannot expect anything but disparity in the length of time served by inmates prior to parole consideration and the volume of persons released to a parole status.

Experience has demonstrated that the best way to obtain proper independence of a parole authority is not by a law saying they are independent, but through the integrity and judgment to retain their independence of any improper pressure. Experience has likewise shown that it is desirable and practicable to make the parole authority a part of the state correctional system or department, without making it subordinate to the administrative head of the department or any other person in parole decisions. Placement in the correctional department points up the mutual responsibility for prison treatment and parole service. The interrelatedness of the correctional process is an accepted fact today. Such administrative placement appears to be desirable from a fiscal and general administrative standpoint. Moreover, the policies and practices of the parole board directly affect both inmate morale in the institution, and the size of the prison population.

The rational organization of a structure is one in which there are clearly defined patterns of activity and in which, ideally, every series of actions is functionally related to the purposes of the organization.[30] According to Gaus, the guiding principle in determining departmental arrangement of state government has been related to that of function.[31] Therefore, this concept substantially has resulted in administrative structures in which relationships are determined by the problems confronted, in which expert knowledge in particular areas is fully utilized, and in which the individual parts contribute to self-preservation and self-realization of the whole program. Yet, in the scheme of correctional services, there is proliferation, and disregard for the totality of the correctional mission.

The injunction to keep the structure of organization "simple, clear, and definite" is often repeated in the literature.[32] The services related to parole administration specifically, and administration of criminal justice services generally, might well follow the injunction.

---

[30]Robert Merton: *Social Theory and Social Structure*. Glencoe, Free Press, 1949, p. 153.

[31]John M. Gaus: The theory of organization in public administration. In *The Frontiers of Public Administration*. Berkeley, Calif., University of California Press, 1936, p. 72.

[32]Griffenhagen and Associates: *Report on General State Organization*. December, 1949, Volume I, Part II, p. 2.

Chapter III

Organization of Personnel For Effective Service

IN THE PREVIOUS CHAPTER, we noted that a substantial amount of parole administration is found in the various boards and commissions charged with that responsibility. In November, 1965, a special Task Force on Correctional Standards was appointed by the staff of the President's Commission on Law Enforcement and Administration of Justice. Its purpose was to select from the standards already published by authoritative bodies those that would be useful to the commission and which were also susceptible to measurement.[1] Correctional standards are defined as the best professional thought concerning the organization and function of a correctional system.

In light of the data presented in Table I, this analysis suggests certain findings. The standard calls for a centralized board, exclusively responsible for decisions on parole release. The consensus suggested that the board should not serve as an advisory body, with parole decisions being made by the governor, the director of correction, or some other administrative officer; and, moreover, should not have the pardon function.[2] The analysis of data suggests that in forty-seven jurisdictions there is, as recommended in the standard, a centralized paroling authority; in four states the parole decision-making process is made by more than

---

[1]These standards are reported in *Correction in the United States: A Survey for the President's Commission on Law Enforcement and Administration of Justice.* New York, National Council on Crime and Delinquency, 1966, pp. 264-280.

[2]*Ibid.*, p .215.

29

one board. The NCCD study found that most parole boards are responsible for certain functions other than parole decision-making.[3] In only one state does the parole board have no responsibility other than parole. Board membership, as was suggested earlier, varies significantly in terms of the number of board members and whether they are full or part-time. Again, the NCCD study reported the data which is found in Table II.

TABLE II

NUMBER OF FULL-TIME AND PART-TIME BOARDS AND
NUMBER OF MEMBERS ACCORDING TO POPULATION

States	Number of Boards			Range in Number of Board Members		
	Full-Time	Part-Time	Combination	Full-Time	Part-Time	Combination
Largest	8	1	1	3-10	7	3
Medium	13	5	2	3- 5	3-6	5-7
Smallest	2	19	0	3- 5	3-6	.. ..
Total	23	25	3	3-10	3-7	5-7

Source: *Correction in the United States.* New York, National Council on Crime and Delinquency, 1966, p. 216.

There is, without question, the prime need to improve the efficiency of parole administration through the appointment of full-time board members (depending on the work load), as well as the establishment of qualifications divorced from politics.

The Problem of Personnel Administration

Our attention now turns to the problems related to staffing. The Task Force on Correctional Standards did not state a preference for one or the other of two administrative structures. In one the parole executive is responsible to the parole board; in the other he is responsible to the department that has general administrative responsibility for the correctional program. "The first form is found in thirty-one states; the second is used in twenty states."[4]

---

[3]*Ibid.*, p. 216.

[4]*Ibid.*, p. 218.

The Function of Organization

All too frequently those engaged in human services become so enamored of the end goal that they give little attention to the means for making that end a reality. Thus, in the social welfare field generally, and in the administration of justice in the specific, where there is a stated enthusiasm for "aiding" the individual, frequently inadequate thought is given to the type of organizational structures that will produce the desired results. A parole system, like any other governmental activity, continuously must be on the alert to see that its organizational structure is so arranged and management programs are so conducted as to make the greatest contribution to the objectives of the system.

Any examination of the organization and management of the parole system would be meaningless if it were limited solely to the scrutiny of the administrative structure now in existence. The best type of organization, one with each unit in its proper place, and with clear lines of responsibility and authority running up and down the hierarchy, can become comparatively worthless if within that hierarchy there is a strong informal organization that bypasses and subverts the formal.[5]

A basic argument for administrative integration of criminal justice services is apparent; that is, the desirability of coordinating state administrative activities. The activities of government should be consistent; the more independent agencies, the greater the possibilities for inconsistency. A rational program of human services activities in state government calls for an integrated, systematic, and rational arrangement of administrative agencies.

To state that a civil service or personnel agency in state government has an influence on personnel management is to state a truism. It may be more to the point to consider to what extent the operations of such an agency tend to improve the sector of parole organization and management. It is extremely difficult to generalize in this matter, for no two states appear to have a relationship of the same order or magnitude between the parole agency and the central personnel system.

---

[5]*Virginia Parole System: An Appraisal of Its First Twelve Years.* A report prepared for the Virginia Parole Board by the Bureau of Public Administration, University of Virginia, Charlottesville, Virginia, May 12, 1955, p. 12.

Professionalism in Corrections

The issue of patronage versus the merit system has become irrelevant in view of the rapid professionalization of the public services. This is not to suggest that patronage no longer exists, but rather that more commonly an attempt is made to maintain some minimal standard of preparation before the individual is favorably considered for a patronage position. An educational profile of adult field personnel has been described by the Louis Harris Survey of Correctional Personnel. While it represents only a sampling, as defined by the Joint Commission on Correctional Manpower and Training, the suggestion remains that university education tends to be reasonably characteristic of those employed at the various levels in the correctional process. Table III presents this data.

It has become apparent that modern, democratic government can function effectively only with a competent, vigorous, and imaginative public service. No matter how efficient the structural foundation, the entire administrative edifice may collapse as a consequence of frustrated human relations and low morale engendered by autocratic supervision and political interference.[6]

Principles for Effective Personnel Administration

Out of this awareness has developed a number of principles which have gained acceptance as criteria in organizing an effective personnel. First, it becomes clear that the responsibility for a dynamic response to public service rests with the chief executive. Stimulating leadership and guidance on his part will provide the inspiration for the most effective attainment for the public program. Second, the chief executive requires an adequate staff organization to assist him in his personnel responsibilities. Such an organization thus becomes a positive tool in administrative management. Third, a public service controlled by patronage and political influence cannot provide the efficient, effective, and economical service that

---

[6]For a discussion of organizational functioning through human relations, see Daniel Katz: Human interrelationships and organizational behavior. In Sidney Mailick and Edward H. Van Ness (Eds.): *Concepts and Issues in Administrative Behavoir.* Englewood Cliffs, N.J., Prentice-Hall, 1962, pp. 166-186. "The ready recruitment of people into a system and the low turnover of those in it are the direct reflection of the attraction of the system as a system." p. 175.

TABLE III
EDUCATIONAL PROFILE OF ADULT FIELD PERSONNEL

	Top Adminis-trators		Supervisors		Functional Specialists	
Eleventh grade or less	....		1%		....	
High school to three years college	13%		14%		13%	
Bachelor's degree	28%		31%		49%	
Sociology		26%		23%		25%
Education		10%		9%		4%
Psychology		10%		14%		14%
Social work		5%		1%		2%
Other		49%		53%		55%
		100%		100%		100%
Graduate study	30%		29%		25%	
Master's degree	27%		24%		11%	
Social work		31%		39%		21%
Education		10%		9%		8%
Psychology		12%		9%		21%
Sociology		19%		26%		17%
Guidance		....		4%		8%
Other		28%		13%		25%
		100%		100%		100%
Ph.D.	1%		1%		1%	
	100%		100%		100%	

Source: Unpublished data from Louis Harris Survey of Correctional Personnel, dated February 21, 1969, from the Joint Commission on Correctional Manpower and Training, courtesy of Dr. B. Frank.

the public taxpayer mandates. Fourth, personnel management cannot be primarily concerned with negative, "police-type" functions. Its primary direction should energize a positive movement to attract and retain the most competent personnel.

Manpower and Manpower Costs

In any state, a very large proportion of expenditures goes for personal services in the form of wages and salaries. There is no exception to this principle in parole administration, where public funds are used principally for salaries, transportation costs, and administrative expenditures for communications and consumable supplies. Relatively speaking, parole and probation services have a lower per capita cost per inmate served, primarily because expenditures are not made for physical plant, maintenance, and care of prisoners, or the operation of a twenty-four-hour, seven-day program. As a consequence, therefore, community field services (including both probation and parole) account for about 15 percent of the annual expenditures for correctional systems, while 85 percent are expended for institutions.

Parole, then, is a major government enterprise financed by a minor expenditure of public funds. In 1966, the National Survey of Corrections found that only 3 percent of all correctional expenditures were directed to parole.[7] In terms of the number of full-time manpower involved, we are really considering a very small number of people. In 1966 that figure was 1,756 parole officers and 243 staff supervisors. The Joint Commission on Correctional Manpower and Training, projecting manpower needs to 1975, suggested that 2,510 parole officers and 315 supervisors would be needed in 1975 if 1965 standards were maintained. If quality standards were to be projected, the figures would increase to 3,270 and 555, respectively. The data is displayed in Table IV.

If agencies are to attain the professional manpower needed to carry out the parole function, it is apparent that there will need to be a major augmentation and reallocation of the expenditure

TABLE IV
PROFESSIONAL MANPOWER IN FELONY PAROLE

	Parole Officers	*Supervisors*
Number employed in 1965	1,888 (includes 132 in institutions, plus some who handle probation as well)	243
Number needed in 1965 to achieve quality standards	2,380 (for parole cases only)	397
Number necessary to maintain 1965 standards in 1975	2,510 (approximately)	315
Number necessary to achieve quality standards in 1975	3,270	555

Source: Unpublished staff document, provided by Dr. B. Frank of the Joint Commission on Correctional Manpower and Training, from its Table M-36, 1969.

---

[7]*Ibid.,* p. 211.

of the criminal justice tax dollar. In Pennsylvania, for example, in 1966 the criminal justice system dollar was divided as shown in Table V.[8]

TABLE V

ALLOCATION OF CRIMINAL JUSTICE TAX
DOLLAR IN PENNSYLVANIA, 1966

Police	.60
Prosecution	.01
Judicial	.07
Institutions	.28
Probation and Parole	.04

Source: Pennsylvania Department of Justice. Figures are for 1966. No later data available.

The Pennsylvania data approximated the findings of the President's Crime Commission as reported in the National Council on Crime and Delinquency Study.[9]

In the National Profile of Corrections, per capita expenditure for selected correctional services is presented by state (although states are not individually identified). That data is summarized in Table VI.

TABLE VI

PER CAPITA EXPENDITURE FOR SELECTED CORRECTIONAL
SERVICES BY STATE POPULATIONS

States	Adult Institutions Range	Parole Range
Small*	.71 - 2.93	.02 - .93
Intermediate†	.26 - 3.11	.01 - .30
Large‡	1.10 - 3.46	.07 - .44

* under 1,000,000 total population.
† between 1,000,000 and 3,500,000 total population.
‡ over 3,500,000 total population.

Source: National Council on Crime and Delinquency: *Correction in the United States*, pp. 233-234.

---

[8]Cf. Pennsylvania Crime Commission: *Task Force Report: Goals for Justice*. Harrisburg, Office of the Attorney General, January, 1969, p. 11.

[9]National Council on Crime and Delinquency: *Correction in the United States, op. cit.*, p. 230.

Recruitment Methods

Obviously, if the projected expansion of personnel ever comes to fruition, positive methods will have to be used to seek out and interest persons qualified by education, training, and experience for correctional work. Moreover, almost all organizations have at least some turnover of personnel, since they tend to outlast the duration of most members' participation, and since they refill some of the vacated positions. Therefore, some organizational means must be devoted to recruitment of new members. This point raises several considerations: (a) How are differences and means of recruitment related to the organization's structure? (b) What are the criteria according to which participants are recruited?

Etzioni[10] suggests three types of organization: coercive,[11] utilitarian,[12] and normative.[13] Means of recruitment differ considerably among the three types. Coercive organizations rely on coercion by the police, military forces, or delegates of the courts. Utilitarian organizations compete for potential recruits in a labor market as they compete for other means of production, through a price mechanism. Typical normative organizations have to rely predominantly on expressive communication and socialization for their lower participants. Professional organizations are the only kind of normative organization which recruits lower participants in part through market competition. But even here recruitment is quite different from that of most utilitarian organizations, since prestige and research or training facilities augment or even outweigh remuneration and related rewards.

This notion would seem to be supported in the research of the Joint Commission on Correctional Manpower and Training, who,

[10]Amitai Etzioni: *A Comparative Analysis of Complex Organizations.* New York, Free Press of Glencoe, 1961, pp. 151-152.

[11]Coercive organizations are organizations in which coercion is the major means of control over lower participants, and high alienation characterizes the orientation of most lower participants to the organization. *Ibid.,* p. 27.

[12]"Utilitarian organizations are organizations in which remuneration is the major means of control." *Ibid.,* p. 31.

[13]"Normative organizations are organizations in which normative power is the major source of control over most lower participants, whose orientation to the organization is characterized by high commitment. Compliance in normative organizations rests principally on internalization of directives accepted as legitimate. Leadership, rituals, manipulation and social and prestige symbols are among the more important techniques of control used." *Ibid.,* p. 40.

in its sample survey, found that job security (66), quality of the program (55), and fringe benefits (45) were more significant factors in the retention of state probation and parole agency field officers than salary (32). Interestingly, proximity to educational facilities (41) and staff development opportunities (35) both rated ahead of financial reward. On the other hand, the preponderance of oratory and the responses from the questionnaire suggested that salary is the principal reason for staff turnover. Table VII presents the Joint Commission study findings.

TABLE VII
FACTORS AFFECTING RETENTION OF STATE
PROBATION AND PAROLE AGENCY FIELD OFFICERS   (N=94)

Factor	Hinders	No Effect	Helps	Don't Know or No Response
Quality of Program	3	21	55	15
Caseloads	35	28	25	6
Salary	36	23	32	3
Hours in work week	13	51	21	9
Job security	4	17	66	7
Fringe benefits	13	28	45	8
Georgraphic location of agency	10	35	35	14
Physical working conditions	16	32	35	11
Promotion opportunities	35	17	34	8
Staff development opportunities	21	29	35	9
Proximity to educational facilities	5	36	41	12
Educational leave	22	26	27	19

Source: Unpublished data, Joint Commission on Correctional Manpower and Training, Table RM-7, March 15, 1969. Courtesy of Dr. B. Frank.

Recruitment has an impact on the quality and effectiveness of any organization. If selection leaves the initial quality of the lower participants "low" (very different from that required by the organizational roles they are expected to carry out, or very different from the end-state the organization is supposed to produce in them), then the effectiveness of the organization tends to be comparatively low. If, on the other hand, the criteria and degree of selectivity ensure that the initial quality of lower participants is "high," effectiveness will be comparatively high, either because resources that would otherwise be required for socialization (i.e., pre-service or in-service training) can be shifted to other tasks, or because the socialization process can carry lower participants closer to the "output" state without increased expenditure of resources.[14] It should be noted, however, that the relationship is not necessarily linear.

An organization may be highly selective in its choice of members, if the population on which it can draw is large enough, and if it is free of other constraints. Thus, the principle thrust should be to produce the maximum base from which choices for new staff could be made.

In general, recruitment for parole staff is handled in several possible ways: (a) by the parole agency itself (b) by the state personnel agency (c) by a joint effort of (a) and (b).

In general, large agencies appear to handle their own recruitment with greater frequency. Characteristically, recruitment activities are a joint effort between the personnel agency (civil service, merit system, or personnel department) and the parole administration unit.

The questionnaire elicited the responses listed in Table VIII.

TABLE VIII
STATE AGENCY HANDLING RECRUITMENT
OF NEW PAROLE STAFF   (N=40)

Agency	Small* (%)	Intermediate (%)	Large (%)
Parole agency	2 (11.5)	2 (25.0)	6 (42.5)
Personnel agency	4 (22.5)	1 (12.5)	1 (7.0)
Joint effort	11 (60.5)	5 (62.5)	7 (49.5)
No response	1 (5.5)	. .	. .

*Small departments: less than 50 field officers and supervisors. Intermediate departments: between 50 and 99 field officers and supervisors. Large departments: more than 100 field officers and supervisors.

Respondents were queried as to the nature of media utilized to publicize the availability of positions, and the need for staff.

In general, larger agencies used a wider variety of recruitment techniques than either small or intermediate agencies. Interestingly, not every agency used the most obvious source of college-level stu-

---

[14]*Ibid., pp.* 157-158.

TABLE IX
MEDIA USED FOR STAFF RECRUITMENT   (N=40)

Technique	Small (%)		Intermediate (%)		Large (%)	
General mailing list	6	(33.0)	3	(37.5)	9	(63.5)
Newspaper advertisement or announcement	12	(66.0)	5	(62.5)	7	(49.5)
Colleges (Career Days with recruiters)	8	(44.0)	6	(75.0)	10	(71.1)
Vacancies listed NCCD	3	(16.5)	.	.	6	(42.5)
Vacancies listed NASW	.	.	.	.	3	(21.0)
Vacancies listed ACA	2	(11.0)	.	.	.	.
Requests to other agencies	1	(5.5)	2	(25.0)	3	(21.0)
Other techniques	4	(22.0)	4	(50.0)	5	(35.0)

dents: college recruitment. The National Council on Crime and Delinquency (NCCD), the American Correctional Association (ACA), and the National Association of Social Workers (NASW) all maintain employment bulletins, yet those resources were virtually unused. Part of the limitation may stem from the range of recruitment activities which are described in Table X.

TABLE X
RANGE OF RECRUITMENT ACTIVITIES   (N=40)

Limits	Small (%)		Intermediate (%)		Large (%)	
State	14	(78.0)	3	(37.5)	4	(28.5)
Region	.	.	4	(50.0)	1	(7.5)
Nation	4	(22.0)	1	(12.5)	9	(64.0)

Recruitment Policy

Recruitment policy, in its stated form, frequently declares the intention that management should seek to find the best man (or woman) for the job. Whatever the agency's intentions, however, such recruitment activities must be consistent with public policy on these matters. Most obvious of these restrictions relate to (a) the residence of the applicant, (b) the age of prospective personnel, and (c) prior criminal involvement.

National policy prohibits discrimination in employment, but actual practice suggests that only a miniscule proportion of the parole officer personnel is recruited from female or minority group ranks.

The impact of restrictive residence requirements for employment has the effect of limiting the agency to filling the jobs with persons with the best possible qualifications from within a given geographic sector, rather than from the larger potential manpower pool. As the data in Table X indicates, small agencies (78%) most often limit their recruitment activities to within the state. On the contrary, large agencies (72%) use regional or national recruitment characteristically. Intermediate size agencies use regional recruitment predominantly (50%) and nationally only to a small extent (12.5).

One of the interesting findings of this study was related to age range limitations imposed by hiring agencies in their recruitment of personnel. Without exception, agencies require that the individual applicant has attained an age beyond his twenty-first birthday. Large agencies indicated a willingness to hire at age twenty-one, but small agencies characteristically seek an individual over twenty-five. This is true also for about half of the intermediate agencies reporting.

The effect of requiring entry age beyond that normally attained at graduation is to eliminate potential workers for whom parole is the first career choice. More specifically, requiring that the individual be twenty-five or older is virtually certain to guarantee that the candidate will have tried another occupational area first and found that he is unsuited to it. More importantly, such policies automatically exclude from immediate appointment those persons who have been specifically trained for the correctional area as part of their university degree work.

TABLE XI
AGE RANGE LIMITATIONS FOR RECRUITMENT

Response	Small (%)	Intermediate (%)	Large (%)
Yes	11 (61)	8 (100)	8 (57)
No	7 (39)	. .	6 (43)

In the following chapter, we shall be looking at manpower selection in parole, with particular reference to the manpower supply.

Chapter IV

Manpower Selection
In Parole

STAFFING IS THE PROCESS of filling jobs in the working organization. For the field of corrections in general, and for parole
services in the specific, leaders have attempted to come to grips
with the basic issues involved in ascertaining manpower needs.
For, regardless of managerial intention to carry out certain defined policies and programs, the fulfillment of stated objectives
can be brought to fruition only when an agency is staffed with
team members to perform the jobs to be done.

The previous chapter concluded with a consideration of the
problems of recruitment. Within the past decade, "a series of
regional and national conferences, limited survey studies, and a
few demonstration programs related to personnel training have
concluded that most correctional institutions and agencies are
clearly understaffed."[1]

With the increase in reported crime in both rural and urban
areas, we can anticipate ultimately a surge of demand for services
from the correctional aspect of the criminal justice system. If law
enforcement makes more arrests, and if more convictions result,
the flow will ultimately reach corrections. And, as Piven and Alcabes point out, ". . . (in) the last stage of the criminal justice
process, parole agencies (will be) assigned rehabilitation and

---

[1]President's Crime Commission: *Task Force Report: Corrections, op. cit.,* p. 93.

control functions in the community with large numbers of offenders newly released from correctional institutions."[2]

Trends in Manpower Supply

One need not labor the point that increases of personnel will be needed just to maintain current ratios between staff and clientele. While field agencies do recruit from a wide variety of educational sources, the most desired choice for academic preparation, according to the Piven-Alcabes study, is social work, followed by corrections.[3]

Only a fraction of these corrections graduates seek careers in parole services.[4] While the graduate output of social work programs is somewhat larger, the entry of such graduates into parole services is minimal. Table XII projects some trends in professional manpower supply and demand as determined by the Joint Commission on Correctional Manpower and Training in 1969.

The magnitude of the manpower problem, then, is one which can be expected to grow, even if current practices are maintained, for the obvious factor of incremental growth in the volume of correctional business. Or, to put it another way, the system will funnel more clientele through it in the ensuing years, and parole is at the end of the funnel. If it is to keep up with the volume of input, it will have to add additional manpower to its operating base. This, of course, raises the question of feasibility of expanding the pool

---

[2] Herman Piven and Abraham Alcabes: *The Crisis of Qualified Manpower for Criminal Justice: An Analytic Assessment with Guidelines for New Policy*. Washington, U.S. Dept. of Health, Education and Welfare; JD Publication No. 564, 1969, vol. I (Probation/Parole), p. 3. In one of the few significant manpower studies published to date, Piven and Alcabes attempt to define a set of guidelines for the development of a national policy regarding probation and parole manpower and training. Unfortunately, in their delineation of the problem, they chose to combine data on probation (which is almost universally county or locally-operated in the U.S.) and parole services (which are always state-operated). Thus, while the problems of manpower may be common to both systems, the strategies for their solution must vary by the nature of the organization and its placement within the scheme of public responsibility.

[3] In the whole of the United States in 1966-1967, there were only forty-seven senior colleges offering degree programs in corrections with a total of 800 graduates.

[4] *Ibid.* Contrast these findings with graduates at the bachelors level in police science and administration. In 1966-1967, there were 473 persons graduated. Charles L. Newman and Dorothy Hunter: Education for careers in law enforcement: an analysis of student output 1964-1967. *Journal of Criminal Law, Criminology, and Police Science,* 59 (1): 139, 1968.

TABLE XII
TRENDS IN PROFESSIONAL MANPOWER SUPPLY AND DEMAND AS
RELATED TO CORRECTIONS: SOCIAL WORKERS AND
SOCIAL WELFARE WORKERS

	In All Settings	In Corrections
Number currently employed	130,000 (includes 26,000 full professionals)	11,560*
Current shortages re: demand	Large shortage, especially those with professional degrees. Est. 12-15,000 vacancies for professionals.	Many vacancies; many positions filled by persons who lack required training.
Current shortages re: quality standards	A need for 50,000 additional *professional* social workers was found in six settings.	20,000
Projected supply to 1975	At most 65,000 professionals. 40-45,000 in 1970. Expected that number employed in social services will be over 200,000 by 1975.	17,000
Projected 1975 shortage re: demand (or maintenance standard)	Would be a shortage of 85,000 professionals for HEW programs alone in 1970.	1,000 approximately
Projected 1975 shortage: quality standards	100,000-125,000	29,500

* This total was figured by classifying two-thirds of the miscellaneous caseworkers (probation, parole, classification, and after-care workers) as social workers. Similarly, shortages were estimated by assuming that two-thirds of the personnel needed in these categories would be drawn from social work or social welfare workers. Those in the remaining one-third were categorized as counselors. Therefore, the estimates of supply and demand for social workers could be increased or decreased to a certain extent by compensators' manipulations of the estimates for counselors.

Source: Unpublished staff document, provided by Dr. B. Frank, Joint Commission on Correctional Manpower and Training. From its Table M-38, 1969.

from which qualified personnel are recruited, selected, and hired, and improving the conditions which will encourage such personnel to remain in the system.

The problem becomes even more apparent when we delineate understaffing in the following terms:

1. The numbers of personnel to do the parole job, as it is currently defined, and in accordance with presently designed expectations; that is, the standards of official public policy.

2. The numbers of personnel to do the job, if the performance

criteria were elevated to the levels of expectation designated by optimal standards for size of caseload, quality and frequency of client contact and related criteria.[5]

In today's complex of jobs, staffing has become a complicated and time-consuming responsibility. The emphasis in the criminal justice system generally has been to upgrade qualifications of undereducated and untrained personnel. But the marketplace does not hold a ready supply of potential personnel—trained or untrained. As Piven and Alcabes point out, the maximum potential manpower pool from schools of social work is limited for the following reasons:

1. Competition comes from other human service areas which are seen as more attractive to social workers.
2. Graduates are not encouraged to practice in correctional settings by their school administrators.
3. Most importantly, the majority of graduates are women (60%) who tend to be excluded from correctional jobs by stated public policy.[6]

Educational Qualifications

There is, of course, overall a large supply of bachelor's and master's degree graduates produced each year from the colleges and universities. In 1966, for example, there were 570,000 bachelor degrees and 133,000 master degrees awarded.[7] If recruitment standards did not pay attention to the area in which graduates were educated, or if graduates from fields foreign to the human services area in general, or corrections in the specific, were to select the administration of criminal justice field for a locus of employment, the problem would be substantially alleviated. But the reality is that correctional administrators report a preference either for social work or corrections-trained graduates; and, commonly, graduates of the non-social science disciplines are seldom attracted to the human services field. Moreover, the relatively low remuneration and the

[5]As defined by NCCD (1968), the Attorney General's Conference on Parole, *op. cit.*, and the American Correctional Association, *op. cit.*

[6]Piven and Alcabes, *op. cit.*, p. 14.

[7]Office of Education, U.S. Department of Health, Education and Welfare: *Projections of Educational Statistics to 1975-76.* Washington, Government Printing Office, 1966, p. 27.

lack of a "professional community" tends to be a barrier to the recruitment of personnel who ordinarily would be among the target recruitment and selection population.

Simply stated, manpower in corrections is an important issue, no matter from which perspective it is viewed. In corrections, staffing patterns in most localities are less advanced than in other human service areas. For example, in the health and welfare fields where personnel shortages are also being experienced, there is consensus on who the fully credentialled professionals are. But no such agreement exists in corrections.[8]

As a consequence, state requirements and actual hiring criteria vary. Some agencies seek staffs with graduate degrees in social work, law, criminology, or psychology. Others seek a college degree with an emphasis on the behavioral or social sciences. An uncomfortably large number of states mandate a high school graduation with either previous experience, or the high school diploma alone as the basis for qualification. Table XIII presents the study findings.

TABLE XIII
EDUCATIONAL QUALIFICATIONS FOR ENTRY LEVEL
PAROLE POSITIONS BY SIZE OF AGENCY

Qualification	Small	Intermediate	Large
High school graduate	0	0	0
High school plus experience	0	1	1
College graduate	12	4	11
College graduate plus experience	1	0	0
Some college or experience	2	3	2

The Standard

The findings in Table XIII should be contrasted with the NCCD Standard for education and experience:

Preferred: A bachelor's degree with a major in the social or behavioral sciences and courses in delinquency and crime *plus* a master's degree from a recognized school of social work, or a

---

[8]Judith G. Benjamin, Marcia K. Freedman, and Edith F. Lynton: *New Role for Nonprofessionals in Corrections: Pros and Cons.* Washington, U.S. Department of Health, Education and Welfare, J.D.-6001 Correction Series, 1966, pp. 2-3.

master's degree in the social or behavioral sciences. Such training is deemed to be full professional training.

Minimum: A bachelor's degree with a major in the social or behavioral sciences and one of the following: (a) one year of graduate study in social work, or in a related field, such as guidance or counseling; or (b) one year of paid experience under professional supervision in a correctional program or recognized social agency.[9]

If judged only against the standard of education and experience, it is abundantly clear that professionalism in terms of academic requirements (to the exclusion of any other criteria) is lacking in the selection process. Additionally, the standard suggests as a minimal requirement:

> The following are basic and irreplaceable requirements for work in the probation and parole field: emotional maturity; integrity; ability to establish effective interpersonal relationships; a firm conviction of the dignity and value of the individual; belief in the capacity of people to change; genuine interest in helping people; intellectual depth; mature judgment; wide experience and the ability to learn from it; continuing interest in improving professionally; and a basic respect for the legal base upon which our society rests.[10]

While the educational and experimental qualities are attainable, the likelihood of finding the foregoing qualities in any one individual is unlikely. In any case, selection practices do not provide for such personality screening in most instances.

Screening Processes

Commonly, the written examination is the primary screening instrument. When the agency wishes to select new staff, either the parole agency, the state personnel agency, or both jointly prepare an examination. Table XIV shows the distribution.

---

[9]National Council on Crime and Delinquency: *Standards for Selection of Probation and Parole Personnel.* New York, The Council, 1968, p. 5. The Professional Council of the NCCD recognizes the standard as in need of continuing revision. In a preamble to the document cited, they state: "The Committee which worked on the revision (i.e., the 1968 revision) does not see the 'Standards' as a finished product, since the entire area of correctional manpower and training is undergoing intensive study, and new concepts are being tested and developed. The work of the Joint Commission on Correctional Manpower and Training will undoubtedly affect existing standards . . . ."

[10]*Ibid.*, p. 4.

TABLE XIV
RESPONSIBILITY FOR PREPARATION OF WRITTEN
EXAMINATION BY SIZE OF AGENCY

Agency Preparing Examination	Small	Intermediate	Large
Parole agency	4	2	3
Personnel agency	8	5	5
Joint effort	4	1	4
No examination	2	0	2

It should be stressed that the written examination can be effective *only* if the process consistently and to a high degree foretells success in the position. Prediction of success or failure depends for accuracy both on knowledge of what elements are most usually associated with successful accomplishment in the position, and in the appropriateness of the criteria for measuring those elements. Personal discussion with parole administrators in various parts of the country have elicited the conclusion that most tests neither predict successful accomplishment nor measure those personal qualities as defined in the NCCD standard.

Success in conducting written tests, then, depends upon the competence of the test technician in planning and framing items which will measure the elements to be tested, and on the selection of relevant elements to be tested. Obviously, two different types of expertise are needed: (a) techniques of testing, and (b) expertness in the subject matter of the position. They are qualities not likely to be combined in a single individual.

As Jucius and others have pointed out, a test is a process of measurement by which it is hoped to determine how well a person has done something or may do in the future.[11]

Thus, the assumption, mostly unvalidated, is that a quantitative score of present knowledge, as measured by the testing instrument, will reveal how a person will function on the job in the future. The absurdity of the position is apparent. As a way, then, of ameliorating the limitations of the testing process, some agencies use either a rated or nonrated oral interview in order to get at some of the dimensions of personality and personal suitability. Some

---

[11]Michael J. Jucius: *Personnel Management,* 6th ed. Homewood, Ill.: Richard D. Irwin, 1967, pp. 166-167.

small number of agencies use neither the written examination nor the professional, rated interview. In those instances, we can speculate that the candidate has passed a test for political reliability, if not for professional competence. Table XV indicates the response to the question regarding written and rated oral examinations.

The Selection Practice

In general, most state parole agencies use some form of competitive procedure for the selection of staff. If a written examination is used (and this was the commonly reported practice), the examination is prepared either jointly by the parole agency and the state personnel agency, or independently by one or the other. More commonly, small agencies reported having the examination independently prepared by the state agency responsible for personnel, while large agencies, in the majority of cases, either did so themselves or participated jointly with the personnel agency in preparing the examination.

TABLE XV
UTILIZATION OF EXAMINATIONS
BY SIZE OF AGENCY

	Written		Oral	
	Yes	*No*	*Yes*	*No*
Small	14	2	12	6
Intermediate	6	0	4	4
Large	14	2	10	4

The preponderance of agencies reporting indicated that they require both the written and the oral examination as part of the selection process. All intermediate size agencies required written exams, though only half required the oral. In only half of the large agencies is the written examination required, but the oral was almost always a part of the selection process.

Among those states which make use of oral examinations, a wide diversity of personnel participate as the oral board. Not uncommonly, the chief administrative officer of the agency participates in the oral examination of new employees. Frequently, the district supervisor or area director has a role in the examination process. Representatives of the state personnel agency, most commonly in small departments, are asked to serve on the oral board. Police officers, judges, university professors, and community members are utilized in some states on oral boards. Obviously, in the assessment of personal characteristics, ability to respond to simulated situations, initial impression of personal stability, and similar characteristics are most readily obtained from the interview situation. The written examination, on the other hand, generally cannot give an assessment of any of those characteristics.

The personal characteristics of the individuals serving on the oral can be significant in the type of information elicited from the candidate. Moreover, the purpose of the oral examination, the subject matter of the interviews, the time limits allowed, the nature of the scoring schedule, and many other factors will have a bearing on the end result. For example, if the oral board composition is primarily composed of persons with social work training, then it is likely that they will approach the interview with the "worker-client" stance. That is to say, they will tend to see and treat the candidate as a whole in relation to his background of family relationships, his cultural heritage, his intellectual capabilities, emotional patterns, and so forth. Service as an examiner would require a contrary stance: to consider personality apart from background, appearance aside from physical fitness. As Klein so candidly states: "To divorce oneself from a well-established habit of seeing around, above, and below an individual and upon request to view him instead in segments or layers is difficult for any social worker, and well nigh impossible for some."[12]

Limitations can be elicited as well from the selective training and perspectives of other disciplines. Lawyers, politicians, bureaucrats, and others each view people from the perspective of their own discipline and interests. The personnel interview in corrections should be for the purpose of rounding out other selective procedures by attention to a previously specified set of factors only. The "intuitive sense" about personnel which some administrators say they acquire after years of experience may be valuable to them as employers but may also be a handicap to them as oral interviewers. Utilizing a "sixth sense" obviously introduces bias into

[12]Alice Campbell Klein: *Civil Service in Public Welfare*. New York, Russell Sage Foundation, 1940, p. 386.

the interview situation by utilizing unconscious reactions to certain characteristics such as appearance, personality, or habit. Factors such as reserve or overassurance in manner may have a "halo" effect beyond their real significance in the oral examination process.

The question of how valuable is the written or oral examination in the selection process remains unanswered, and may be unanswerable. We do not know, for example, to what extent the written examination fails to provide opportunities for the truly educated individual to demonstrate his knowledge, or if the oral examination stifles the originality of the imaginative candidate.

MacKinnon, writing on the identification and development of creative personnel, points out that a certain amount of intelligence is required for one to be creative; but beyond that point, being more or less intelligent does not determine the level of a person's creativeness.[13] He goes on to suggest that creative persons are independent in thought and action and are not especially well-rounded. Generally, they have one-sided interests, sharp edges to their personalities, and marked peaks and dips on their personality tests profiles.[14] It should go without saying that creativity should be nurtured in the human services area. The extent to which standard personnel selection processes eliminate the creative individual is an unknown quantity. We can speculate, however, that in many instances the truly creative individual is excluded in the hiring process because he is considered to be too risky and dangerous an undertaking.

A similar criticism has been leveled against the selection process in business by John Cunniff.[15] In its utilization of mass-produced employment tests, it was found that valuable talent was being lost. Not infrequently, an applicant who cannot perform well on a test might perform well on the job. Illustrations of the reverse situation are well known in every agency. Thus, Cunniff argues on more reliance on the personal examination. As was indicated

[13]Donald W. MacKinnon: The identification and development of creative personnel. *Personnel Administration, 31*(1):8, 1968.

[14]*Ibid.*, p. 9 *ff.*

[15]John Cunniff: Employment tests deprive business of good workers. *Reporter Dispatch, 52*(18):18, March 25, 1968.

earlier, however, the same exclusionary bias can prevail if the oral examiner fails to recognize either the talents or the potentialities of the candidate.

Other Selection Factors: Health

The fundamental personnel objective of the correctional system should be the selection of qualified persons who are interested in correctional service as a career.[16] Presumably, in addition to the rating of individual qualifications from the standpoint of prior education, training, personality, and experience, one might expect that the factor of the candidate's health would be evaluated. Such was not the case, however. Cumulatively, only six of the reporting agencies, the majority from small agencies, required a preliminary health examination. No intermediate-sized agency required a preliminary physical. Beyond the accustomed variations in agency practice, it is difficult to account for the failure to utilize health as a screening factor. There can be no doubt that health factors can bear significantly on work performance. Admittedly, the parole job is not an arduous one as compared with the police role. But, as Mosher and Kingsley indicate: "The preentry examination not only sifts out those who have a contagious disease or are physically below par and constitute a definite employment risk, but also discovers defects of one sort or another that should be considered in the placement process."[17]

Residence Requirements

Competitive examinations for entry into the correctional service should be open to all citizens of the United States without regard to residence.[18] One of the more significant findings of this study was that agencies create part of their manpower problem by limiting selection of personnel to those who reside within their own state boundaries.

In general, these restrictions are not limited to the correctional

---

[16]American Correctional Association: *Manual of Correctional Standards, op. cit.,* p. 173.

[17]William E. Mosher and J. Donald Kingsley: *Public Personnel Administration.* New York, Harper and Brothers, 1941, p. 601.

[18]American Correctional Association: *Manual of Correctional Standards, op. cit.,* p. 173.

TABLE XVI
RESIDENCE REQUIREMENTS FOR INITIAL APPOINTMENT

	Small	Intermediate	Large
None	9	8	10
One year or less	3	0	2
One to two years	3	0	1
Other	3	0	1

field. In the vast majority of cases, either the civil service law, the rules of the commission, or political expediency restricts the selection of personnel to residents of the state. But the fact remains that the demands for a staff engaged in providing complex services cannot uniformly be met within a restricted area of selection. Such restriction is one of the ever-present banes of the correctional service.

References and Fingerprints

Part of the selection process in most agencies involves the collection and evaluation of personal and experience references, the requirements varying from two to six or more. As a general rule, references are obtained for two purposes: (a) to get at such intangibles as character, integrity, or personality, and (b) as a means of verifying or corroborating information presented by the applicant. In neither respect are references a very satisfactory device, since no candidate is likely to give as reference a person whose testimony might prove unfavorable or embarrassing. The reliability of references can be enhanced by personal investigation. Both correspondence and personal investigation, as well as fingerprint checks, are utilized by some agencies. There is no uniformity as to how the personal investigation is carried out, or by whom it is done: the operating department or the state personnel agency. Again, as agencies have limited resources, and personal investigations tend to be rather expensive aspects of the selective process, we can speculate that in many instances the investigative process tends to be a superficial one.

The position taken by Mosher and Kingsley in regard to personal investigations is one worthy of support. They state:

As in other instances of rating, opportunity should be provided for appeal in respect to the rating developed by personal investigation. This means that the candidate should have the opportunity of knowing the character of any damaging evidence secured against him and of filing an answer to it. That is of utmost importance. Unless it is scrupulously observed, the potential dangers in an investigational procedure may outweigh all the advantages.[19]

Table XVII presents the picture in regard to the requirements for references and fingerprints.

TABLE XVII
ELIGIBILITY FACTORS: REFERENCES AND FINGERPRINTS

	References		Fingerprints	
	Yes	*No*	*Yes*	*No*
Small	18	0	8	10
Intermediate	7	1	3	5
Large	11	3	10	3

Veterans Preference

Preferential treatment of certain individuals has been institutionalized in most states, not only for the corrections system, but for all public positions. Over two-thirds of small agencies, and almost all intermediate or large agencies granted some form of veteran preference. The range of special consideration included additional points on examinations to absolute preference for disabled veterans in some jurisdictions.

The tradition of granting special privilege to ex-soldiers dates back to the Civil War, "entitling them to a preference for employment against other persons of equal qualifications for the place."[20]

It is extremely difficult to gauge the effect of veterans' preference upon the manpower situation, or upon the quality of service performed generally. In an area when military service has almost become universal for all able-bodied men, the notion of providing special consideration for veterans becomes questionable. The issue will not be pursued here, however, since the likelihood of any change in the practice in the foreseeable future is extremely remote.

---

[19]*Op. cit.*, p. 228.

[20]Lewis Mayers: *The Federal Service, A Study of the System of Personnel Administration of the United States Government.* New York, Macmillan, 1922, p. 406 *ff*.

Employment of Former Offenders

Daniel Glaser, in his important study of the effectiveness of a prison and parole system, writes:

It is an anomalous situation that men are employed by the federal and state governments to devote a major portion of their time to persuading private employers to hire ex-prisoners; yet these governments themselves are extremely reluctant to hire men who have been in prison. Although government agencies frequently have taken the leadership in the employment of other types of handicapped persons, they lag behind private industry in employment of men who have a criminal record.[21]

Glaser's statement is supported by the findings of this study. Inquiry was made as to the exclusionary dimensions of a prior arrest record and for a prior conviction. The data is presented in Table XVIII.

TABLE XVIII
PRIOR ARREST OR CONVICTION AS A BAR TO EMPLOYMENT

	Prior Arrest		*Prior Felony Conviction*	
State	*Yes*	*No*	*Yes*	*No*
Small	6	12	15	3
Intermediate	4	4	7	1
Large	1	13	7	7

It is apparent from this data that parole systems exclude from their personnel complement individuals who have had valuable experience as participants in the criminal justice system. If the success of the Alcoholics Anonymous Program in the community can be attributed to the utilization of controlled alcoholics as therapists, then it can be postulated that the former offender may have an important role to play in the parole rehabilitation process. As matters stand at present, however, it is unlikely that such a person would be employed in the parole system, whatever his potential contribution.

---

[21]Daniel Glaser: *The Effectiveness of A Prison and Parole System*. Indianapolis, Bobbs-Merrill, 1964, p. 414. A variety of demonstration programs for manpower development and training are reported by the Manpower Administration of the U.S. Dept. of Labor. Interestingly, of twelve projects reported through January, 1969, none related itself to the preparation of offenders to take on criminal justice jobs. U.S. Dept. of Labor: *Manpower Development and Training in Correctional Programs*. Washington, MDTA Experimental and Demonstration Findings No. 3, 1968, p. 199.

Summary

In summary, this chapter examined a number of factors related to manpower selection in the parole service. Consideration was given to the elements of the selection technique involving the written and oral examination, as well as the potentials for target manpower groups from social work and corrections training programs. In the study, a wide variety of practices was elicited in regard to the appointment process, as well as to the finding that a prior arrest and prior conviction is a bar to employment in the parole service.

In the next chapter, we shall examine the induction process for the parole officer and the processes which prepare him as an agent of the system.

Chapter V

Induction and Training Of Personnel

T HE ROLE OF THE PAROLE OFFICER is a diverse one which requires a comprehensive grounding in both casework skills and investigative techniques. These skills must be utilized in the three broad areas of supervision which include the following:

1. *Case assistance* and the development and use of community resources, including counseling, group work, job finding, and special placement efforts.
2. *Control,* including case observation, surveillance, and arrest, when necessary.
3. *Decision-making,* especially in areas which affect the legal status of the parolee.[1]

Thus, the agent must perform the following tasks:

1. Closely observe the parolee's behavior in order to gain some insight into the nature of his (the parolee's) problems.
2. Assist in improving the offender's social and emotional adjustment through the use of techniques directed to individual and group counseling strategies.
3. Arrange for specialized intensive intrapsychic help when indicated.
4. Provide or initiate specialized assistance where needed in such sectors as vocational or marital adjustment.

---

[1]California Department of Corrections: *A Report to the Legislature on the Work Unit Parole Program.* Sacramento, California Department of Corrections, December, 1968, p. 3.

5. Make appropriate referrals for legal, educational, medical, religious, and financial assistance.
6. Investigate alleged or known criminal activity by the parolee.
7. Maintain specialized controls, such as antinarcotic testing and surveillance.
8. Make arrests and place parolees in confinement, when necessary.
9. Report and make recommendations to the paroling authority.[2]

All of these roles call for an individual who is well trained at the point of induction into the parole service. He must be provided with an opportunity to keep abreast of the developments in his field of professional practice. The former standard is obtained through the maintenance of a high standard of pre-service education.[3] The latter occurs through the following:

1. Leaves of absence for educational purposes.
2. Participation in intramural staff development and external training programs, institutes, and workshops.
3. The availability and accessibility of a professional library.
4. Provision of capable direction by qualified supervisors and managerial personnel.
5. The maintenance of evaluative performance research activity in the agency.
6. An agency philosophy which encourages creativity and new approaches in dealing with old problems, rather than a rigid doctrinaire policy of *status quo.*

The Volume of the Parole Agent Task

The most recent accounting of the number of persons on parole in the United States was identified in the report of the President's Commission on Law Enforcement and the Administration of Justice. In 1965-66, the number given was 102,036, under supervision of 1,756 parole officers.[4] Caseloads range from 37 to 245 in states where caseloads are mixed (i.e. both probation and parole cases

---

[2]*Ibid.*
[3]To be discussed in Chapter VI.
[4]President's Crime Commission: *Task Force Report: Corrections, op. cit.,* p 189.

are in the same caseload) and from 40 to 93 in states with separate parole caseloads.[5]

The Office Assignment of the Parole Agent

In general, the parole officer, when he is employed and assigned to a working location, finds himself either working alone or in a small office with four or fewer co-workers. While there are regional variations, three out of four parole office locations are staffed by four or fewer parole officers. The distribution below is based on survey data from the Joint Commission on Correctional Manpower and Training.

TABLE XIX

DISTRIBUTION OF PAROLE OFFICE
LOCATIONS BY NUMBER OF OFFICERS (%)

Number of Officers	Distribution of Office Locations				
	East	*Midwest*	*South*	*West*	*Total*
1	42%	47%	47%	27%	44%
2 to 4	30	22	40	26	32
5 to 7	12	6	8	17	9
8 to 10	5	2	2	18	5
11 to 15	3	3	2	8	3
16 to 20	4	1	1	3	1
More than 20	4	19	..	1	6
Total	100%	100%	100%	100%	100%

Source: Unpublished data from the Joint Commission on Correctional Manpower and Training. Staff working document Table M-39(B), March 17, 1969. Data courtesy of Dr. B. Frank.

Such manpower distribution dictates that the officer must be able to operate with considerable autonomy, principally since in all probability he is, in fact, alone. In order to achieve the desired professional upgrading, as was suggested earlier, the individual should be given the opportunity for educational leave with some agency support, either in the form of salary, tuition, or both. The survey data show that, except for several states, neither salary nor tuition aid is available. The shocking part of this discovery is related to the fact that twenty-one states either have no minimum

---

[5]*Ibid.*

educational requirements, or have established high school graduation as the entry requirements.[6]

Frequency of In-Service Training

Study data further support the Crime Commission findings of the neglect of in-service training.[7] Wide variations were found in all states reporting as to the frequency of in-service training activity, and the person or persons responsible for its promulgation. No qualitative determination was attempted for the apparent reason that measures of quality or effectiveness are not employed.

Training Personnel

However, a part of this study was directed to the determination of whether there existed in the parole field agencies a position title which related to a staff development or training position. In limited instances, such a position did exist, although the title varied among the states. In general, the training position was most frequently absent in small departments, though not to the exclusion of the larger ones. In fact, almost half of the large agencies reported no training officer position.

Consistent with the lack of a training officer position was the concomitant lack of funds specifically budgeted for staff training. Generally, training funds were drawn from regular operating budgets and, as a consequence, represented a remainder from other activities, rather than a basic commitment on the part of the agency or the state government to the training function.

In most states, the study elicited the fact that administrative

---

[6]These findings were affirmed by the President's Crime Commission: *Task Force Report: Corrections, op cit.*, p. 190, as well as from data obtained in this study. The current study is not in accord with the Crime Commission finding that thirty states require a minimum educational requirement of a college degree. Study data indicate, in many instances, that combinations of "some" college and related experience is frequently stated as an alternative to college graduation. While stressed in the standards, and widely acknowledged as desired, less than half of the states maintain minimum educational qualifications.

[7]In its study report, the President's Crime Commission found that approximately 55 percent of parole agencies reported having regular in-service training programs. However, when there was a division made as to frequency of in-service training, the distribution was as follows: weekly, 3.6 percent; monthly, 21.4 percent; quarterly, 7.1 percent; annually, 28.6 percent; other, 39.3 percent. *Task Force Report: Corrections, op. cit.*, p. 198.

and supervisory personnel carry continuing responsibility both for the orientation of new staff and for the development of in-service and staff development activities.

Similarly, most states reported that they maintained some sort of formal staff in-service training, as well as a procedure for initial orientation of new staff. The information collected, though occasionally detailed, was of insufficient quality to ascertain either the content or breadth of the training experience.

The Nature of Induction Training

Irrespective of the type of educational preparation an individual may have had before he seeks a position in a correctional agency, we may rightly assume that he comes with very little knowledge of the fundamental mechanics of agency operation. In the United States, probation and parole agencies and correctional institutions often provide an orientation period and an "apprenticeship," with the subsequent assignment of the new worker to an experienced officer who will continue the orientation process. Some of these programs are formally organized and can be quite valuable to the new worker, not only in terms of providing procedural information, but also in providing a general orientation to the philosophy and goals of the agency. Obviously, some post-entry programs (or perhaps more properly "beginning service" training) are more effectively developed than others. All too frequently, however, the new employee is not given any meaningful instruction beyond an exposure to the "rule book" and is sent forth essentially as a free agent in an unsuspecting society.

Elsewhere, departmental training programs are doing a fine job, not only in creating a professional image for their personnel, but also instructing them in the basic mechanics of providing effective service to correctional clients and to the community.

The length of the post-entry training period should depend upon a variety of factors, not least among which is the ability and demonstrated capacity of the new worker. A coherent "core" program, however, must be established for all new staff. This "core" post-entry training program in the correctional field should include an exposure to the various social resources of the community and region, agency visitation, and exposure to law enforcement personnel and practices, and visits to correctional facilities for juveniles and adults in the region. Post-entry training should continue throughout the individual's tenure in the agency, bringing him up to date on changes in agency policy and operation, as well as seeking out his thinking on proposed policy changes.

Most states reported that their in-service training programs include field officers, supervisors, and administrators. It is not unreasonable to assume that, in the absence of formally constructed programs, supervisors and administrators are present, but not in the role of "learners."

Evaluation of In-Service Training

Although it is relatively easy to ascertain the costs of training, it is often much more difficult to determine its true value. However, if training is to be conducted as efficiently and effectively as possible, then some method of evaluating such training must be developed by the participating agency.

The responsibility for the development of such methods is usually given to the person responsible for the training. Inherent in such an arrangement is the apparent lack of objectivity which might stem from a person having to be critical of his own activity. Moreover, such evaluation may degenerate into an attempt merely to justify.

Ideally, the agency can refer the questions related to the evaluation of training programs to the planning and research unit of the department. In the absence of such a unit, consultation and the actual work itself can generally be obtained from a university or college nearby which frequently has a person competent to take on such responsibility.

Diamond suggests that we start out with the underlying assumption that training is inherently good, and that evaluation consists of seeking ways to make it even better.[8]

While such a positive notion is meritorious, much of what passes for training is hardly more than exhortation to perform more effectively under adverse conditions, and to decry the lack of public

---

[8]Harry Diamond: Factors in planning and evaluating in-service training programs. *Journal of Criminal Law, Criminology, and Police Science, 53*:505, December, 1962.

understanding, adequate finances, and appropriate judicial or police behavior.

It is often extremely difficult to determine the effectiveness of in-service training, and guidelines must be developed in order to ascertain the true worth of a training program. As Diamond[9] has pointed out, there are four aspects which should be carefully examined and measured:

1. The reaction of the trainee. It should be determined how the trainee feels about a recently completed training program. A sheet should be provided for him to record his reactions anonymously. The questionnaire should be easy to fill out and space provided for additional comments. In evaluating this reaction sheet, it should be kept in mind that just because a trainee "liked" the program (and the opportunity to break away from the job for a time), may not be a good index of its true worth. Rather, the evaluator should be able to sift through the responses and determine if the training *itself* has real value for the trainee.

2. What the trainee has learned. What did the trainee learn as a result of the training program? To determine this, he should be tested before and after the training experience to find out just how much of the training material he has understood. These tests could be a combination of written tests and question-and-answer sessions with the evaluator.

3. Changes in the trainee's behavior. The basic goal of any training program is to change the behavior of the trainee in a given area. He may readily absorb the training materials intellectually, but never put them into practice.[10] Before a behavior change can take place, the trainee must want to change his behavior; he must know what behavior needs modification; and he must be given the time and ample opportunity on the job to effect these changes. He should be tested before and after the training experience, with adequate time elapsing between for any behavior changes to occur.

---

[9]*Ibid.*, pp. 505-506.

[10]One should recall also Pfiffner's warning, "It is not very difficult to bring about intellectual acceptance of human relations concepts and principles, but the person who expresses such acceptance may go back to the work situation and revert to his former bad habits." John M. Pfiffner: *The Supervision of Personnel.* Englewood Cliffs, N.J., Prentice-Hall, 1958, p. 458.

4. The achievement of results. All effective training programs begin with the basic question: "What is it we want to accomplish?" Only then can effective training materials and methods be formulated to accomplish these stated goals. In order to determine the success of the training program, the evaluator must first analyze that aspect of agency performance requiring modification and determine the level of performance before the training occurs. Then, after the training experience, further analysis will determine what changes were actually brought about. Even so, it is not always entirely clear whether these changes were brought about as a result of the training alone. In the effort to determine the value of a given training program, care must be taken in analyzing an imperfect instrument, at best.

The Strategy for Post-Entry Training

As was indicated earlier, in-service or post-entry training involves not only a concentrated exposure to the mechanics of agency rules and practice, but also an opportunity to identify with the community in which service is to be rendered. It must be structured in such a way as to enhance a unified view of the correctional process, rather than to compartmentalize the individual in a single and unrealistic view of the totality. It is, again, structured to meet the needs of the individual for more effective job performance and the personal satisfaction which will ultimately evolve.[11]

The usual arrangement for training new staff simulates on-the-job training. The characteristic plan for orienting new staff is for the new parole officer to report to his assignment, where he is received either by a district supervisor or a more experienced officer who is responsible for inducting him into his job responsibilities. Orientation outlines, either specific or general, are sometimes available to serve as instructional guides. At some time during the probationary period, the new worker may visit the state office of the agency, where he is introduced to the state personnel and learns more regarding the overall state operation. Not uncommonly, this exposure to the central office precedes the field experience.

The usual problem encountered in this method of orientation is

---

[11]Jane K. Ives: Basic training for probation officers. *Social Work.* 8:51-58, July, 1963.

that the local supervisor, already overburdened with duties and responsibilities, finds it extremely difficult to devote much time to the slow and sometimes painful process of teaching the new officer the many facets of the job. Survey experience has demonstrated that even where well-defined plans are available, when emergencies arise, the new worker's schedule is the first to be adjusted to provide the needed time.[12]

Not uncommonly, supervisory personnel lack the skill to teach, and with the heavy pressures of the daily work, the new worker is given too much, too fast. As a consequence, the new parole officer often learns the job in a fragmentary fashion. In the words of one administrator, "There is a great temptation to give the new worker a manual and a caseload and hope for the best."

Funding as a Problem

Notwithstanding the problems which have just been described, field agencies see training as an important function of their organization. But, as with so many other elements of parole administration, funding continues to be a critical problem. Almost universally, among small, intermediate and large departments, the practice in relation to staff participation in conferences, professional meetings, and such was subject to the availability of budgeted funds. In general, unless the meeting is located close to the agent, he does not get to participate. This is especially true of meetings of national professional organizations.

Graduate Training

While several sectors of the human services area, notably child welfare, mental health, and public welfare, have encouraged personnel to seek graduate professional education and have provided subsidy for such educational activity, such practices are uncommon in the adult parole field. None of the intermediate departments provided such opportunity, and a limited number of small and large departments provided either tuition, subsidy, or both. Equally discouraging was the finding that the majority of agencies not now

---

[12]Based on the author's personal experience in consultation. Similar experiences have been reported by staff consultants of NCCD.

providing advanced educational opportunities had not made efforts to secure funds for such a program. In other words, these agencies neither had such interest in educational advancement, nor attempted to provide opportunities by seeking to secure funds either through public or private auspices.

Effect of the Law Enforcement Education Program

Under the terms of recent federal legislation, provision is made for the granting of funds to personnel employed in law enforcement agencies (generically described to include police, courts, and correctional services) in order to upgrade the quality of educational attainment.[13]

It is still too soon to determine the impact of this funding source on educational practices of personnel employed in parole agencies, or in any of the law enforcement sectors, for that matter. Ideally, with the removal of the burden of tuition costs, personnel will be more inclined either to complete undergraduate work, or enter into advanced educational programming. In large measure, how staff will use such funds will depend upon agency policy, which could either encourage, through the use of release time, or discourage, by its denial, a general upgrading of educational attainment by incumbent staff.

Educational Leave

A finding of the study indicated that five of the large states had institutionalized educational leave programs for professionalization of staff. Typical of such policy is the New York state program, which was instituted almost a decade ago. Rules and regulations for this program are included as an Appendix to this study, since they represent a viable philosophic and operational approach to the professionalization of staff.[14]

---

[13]Public Law 90-351, "Omnibus Crime Control and Safe Streets Act." This Act is designed to assist state and local governments in reducing the incidence of crime, to increase effectiveness, fairness, and coordination of law enforcement and criminal justice systems at all levels of government. The academic assistance provisions (Sec. 406) provides for loans and grants for educational purposes.

[14]See Appendix B.

Professional Library Resources

In the absence of a regular in-service training program, or staff development opportunities by way of educational leave, or conference and workshop participation, the availability of professional literature for self-improvement provides an alternative strategy to achieve similar ends. Study data elicited the finding that in at least one-third of the small departments, a professional circulating library was neither available to field staff, nor that library collections were available in district or regional offices. In general, such collections were available in intermediate and large departments, although exceptions could be noted in both areas.

The study findings did not attempt to appraise either the quality of the library holdings, the ease of access and availability, or the frequency of usage by staff. Based, however, on an earlier informal study by the author, it can be concluded that such collections tend to stay in central offices, and that staff is frequently unaware that such literature is available for their use.[15]

Conclusion

The problems of induction and training of personnel in adult parole systems are manifold. In large measure, agencies lack the personnel, the funds, and, in some instances the policy, to develop sound beginning and post-entry training programs. In large measure the resources which are available have not been utilized. In these states where the mechanisms have been developed which bring the field agency and the university into a working partnership, both institutions have benefited. It is a model which other states might well emulate. The next chapter examines the role of the university in relation to the preparation of personnel for the criminal justice area.

---

[15]Unpublished notes, based on twenty in-service training programs with adult parole officers, 1957-68.

Chapter VI

The University and
The Parole System

IN-SERVICE TRAINING should not be designed to duplicate the educational program of the university. The basic job of staff training belongs to the agency, although there are many ways in which the agency can make use of college and university faculties in the training of parole staff. In a sense, universities should recognize the potential symbiotic relationship which could be developed between the faculties and the personnel of the various correctional services.[1] The agency can provide for the university the viable experiences for research, program evaluation, and student learning opportunities, while the university can provide both the skilled manpower and the students who will share in the opportunities which the agency can make available.

Obviously, no university or combination of universities can hope regularly to involve all employed personnel in the criminal justice system. The universities can, and do, provide conferences, institutes, and workshops which can contribute to the development of the individual in the performance of his job.

But, in the final analysis, unless the agencies and services to which these people return can accommodate to the new dimensions within which the trainee has been stimulated to operate, the training experience can become wasted and an exercise in frustration.

---

[1]Some of the ways in which this can be accomplished are described in Charles L. Newman and Theodore Vallance: Higher education and state government: opportunities for cooperation in the administration of justice. *Attorney General's Bulletin* (Pennsylvania), *3*(2):19-23, 35, 1969.

There must be firm commitment, then, on the part of operating agencies to examine their functions, policies, and procedures and make the necessary changes if they want the benefit of staff training and the most modern and effective strategies to accomplish given ends. By the same token, however, it behooves the university offering the training to be knowledgeable about the needs of the agency for training and their opportunities for putting it to use.

The need for such examination of objectives and means extends also to the employment of persons who are products of the university enterprise at the various degree levels. Unless the agencies are willing to make use of the talents, skills, and knowledge which the professionally prepared new entrant brings with him to the field, the prospect of keeping such a person in the system is substantially reduced. Under such circumstances, both the agency and the university are losers, since the preparation may go unused and the agency loses a potential talent source.

A wide variety of disciplines are involved in the preparation of personnel for the various sectors of the criminal justice system. Ordinarily, we are inclined to think only in terms of the skills related to law enforcement and correctional treatment personnel. But the justice field uses a broad variety of other personnel, including teachers, psychologists, and statisticians.

Specifically, there are different types of educational and training contributions which a university can make in cooperation with the justice field agencies, both to upgrade staff performance and to enhance agency effectiveness. These are:[2]

   1. Pre-entry education: university-based with agency involvement.

     a. Degree programs

     b. Certificate (1 year)

     c. Associate (2 years)

     d. Bachelors (4 years)

     e. Advanced (variable)

---

[2]*Ibid.*, p. 21; see also Piven and Alcabes: *op. cit.*; U.S. Children's Bureau: *Training Personnel for Work with Juvenile Delinquents* (1954); *Career Education in the Correctional Field* (report of an institute at the Pennsylvania State University, 1963); and the several publications of the Joint Commission on Correctional Manpower and Training, specifically *Criminology and Corrections Programs: A Study of the Issues* (1968), *Targets for In-Service Training* (1967), and a consultant paper, Kenneth Polk: *The University and Corrections: Potential for Collaborative Relationships* (1969).

f. Internships
2. Post-entry (in-service): joint agency and university involvement.
   a. Academy
   b. Agency-based school
   c. Agency-university cooperative program for recruits
   d. Conferences, workshops, and institutes
   e. Training "packages"
   f. Consultation
   g. Testing for entry
3. Staff and executive development: university with agency or inter-agency groups.
   a. Seminars
   b. Credit and non-credit courses
   c. Exchange of personnel programs
   d. Inter-service workshops
   e. Consultation
   f. Testing for promotion
   g. Trainer development

Pre-Entry Education

Pre-entry education and training are those aspects of professional preparation which involve the person seeking a career opportunity in the corrections field.

We are just starting to recognize the problems we face in the preparation of individuals for the correctional field. At this point, no academic area has the patent on the best pedagogic method. Political science, psychology, sociology, and legal education leave much to be desired in their educational models. A pattern of education which stresses applicational designs on a strong science base, coupled with practicum experience, provides a better fit to meet some needs of the correctional field. Much of what has been taught on the graduate level (as, for example, in social work) could be handled quite well by undergraduates, especially since the quality of undergraduate students has improved so markedly in recent years.

In keeping with this notion of professional preparation, it should be recognized that there are levels and degrees of intensive preparation. One does not need four years of postgraduate training in medicine in order to do the highly necessary functions of a medical laboratory technician. Yet, one does need a type of intensive preparation based upon the specific definition of the role that the individual plays in the treatment process. Thus, any notion of professional education of the person for the field of corrections must be clearly tied to the role and responsibility that the individual will carry within the field. We are making some progress in that direction through the various standards which are being drawn for the field. But, in large measure, the role definition of the parole officer will have to come from the field.

Education creates preparation, but preparation must serve the needs of the field. Thus, as has been stated previously, there is a joint responsibility where the field and the university jointly share the responsibility for creating an educational experience which will have both utilitarian and broad social value. There is a growing emergence of this pattern in all phases of education—in the social as well as the physical sciences. It should not mean that the correctional field controls the direction of education, nor that education controls the field—but rather that they mutually recognize the joint responsibility for the preparation of people for their occupational mission and as community members.

Part of the issue today, in terms of what type of education is necessary, hinges on the lack of agreement on the sensitivity of specific correctional roles. If the parole officer functions as a data collector, then he needs one level of training. If he is essentially an independent treatment person, with a great deal of decision-making responsibility, then a different intensification of training is necessary. This should lead us, then, to recognize that the content of preparation should be predicated upon the role definition and performance expectation of the parole agent.

In keeping with the idea of levels of professional education and preparation, there are some materials which cannot be adequately covered in the four-year period allotted to the undergraduate preparation of the individual. Admittedly, some individuals will lack either the inclination, ability, or interest to go beyond that point. Others will seek a more sensitive role in the structure of their profession, and, as a consequence, will need more advanced training.

A Model for Correction Education
At the Four-Year Level

In this educational model it is assumed that the person entering the law enforcement-corrections area needs a strong base (core content) which is parallel to that provided to students concerned with the social and behavioral science areas, except that the educational content must be organized in such a fashion as to give an applicational focus to content.

In order to assure the broadest coverage which the bachelor's degree denotes, it is vital that the following content be included in the four-year curriculum:[3]

1. Organization of Government. The content this area will be concerned with is local, state, and national government, with particular emphasis upon the place of law in the operation of governmental activities. The content would also include a concern with the political structure of society and the role of government in economic activity, including a consideration of the sources and allocation of governmental finances, government as a controller, government as a provider, and government as a regulator.

2. The Organization of Society. This content should be related to an understanding of American society from a structural functional frame of reference. In addition, consideration should be given to role, status, culture, class, community, neighborhood, mobility, social problems, race relations and minorities, historical antecedents of Western society, and deviance from a societal perspective.

3. Organization of the Human Personality. The life cycle (conception through senescence) should be considered, both from a biophysical and a social psychological perspective. Both normal and abnormal behavior, with special reference to the law violator, would be stressed in the course content.

4. Communications Area. The content should produce skills in written and verbal communication, public information, and report writing.

5. Concept Formation. This content should provide an aware-

---

[3]This model is now in use at the Pennsylvania State University, Law Enforcement and Corrections program, as developed by the author.

ness of the logical processes, identification of problems, the scientific method, and the quantification and analysis of data.

6. *Clinical Processes Area.* This area would provide technical skill in interviewing, treatment models related to the enhancement of social functioning, control of deviant behavior and the role of the change agent, as well as the array and distribution of human welfare services.

7. *The Administration of Justice.* This area would be concerned with agencies involved in the progression of the accused from arrest to (offender) release, crime-producing and controlling factors in society, the offender in the justice system, the rights of the individual under due process, and the strategic application of the correctional apparatus.

8. *Skill Areas.* Appropriately placed at intervals within the four-year curriculum there should be a series of practicum (i.e. internship) courses related to law enforcement, correctional field services, and institutional settings. The practicum, if properly designed, will reinforce the didactic classroom material, and provide an opportunity for the individual to test out, on an applied basis, the conceptual material he has learned. Each student would then have experienced three different settings, so that he will have exposure to the full array of services within the administration of justice cycle. Thus, the student will have an awareness and appreciation of those services which precede and/or follow his area of occupational interest and choice. Through the rotation, the individual will have a more professional relationship than he would if his exposure were limited to a single setting. The contribution of the field agency to this sector of the educational program is obvious.

Post-Entry Education

As has been mentioned earlier, irrespective of the type of educational preparation an individual may have had, we may rightly assume that he comes to the agency with very little knowledge of the particulars of agency operation. The administration and operation of such basic programs are primarily an agency responsibility. The university, however, can make a major contribution to such entry-level programs, through the provision of tested training "packages," consultation on educational strategies, and direct input into the organization and/or teaching program. Then, at regular periods for the first several years of employment, the employee can be exposed to a series of increasingly more complex levels of training, the structure and operation of which can be shared by agency and university personnel in the various areas of professional competence. Other important responsibilities which the university can share in are such areas as the development of tests which measure entry and promotional capacities, training of the trainers, and pre- and post-training evaluation strategies.

Staff and Executive Development

Basically, the function of staff and executive development programs is to stretch the latent capacity of the worker so that the can (a) do a better job for the agency and the community; (b) gain more job satisfaction through finding more effective and efficient ways of performing his job; (c) generate a better understanding of the function of his job and agency in relation to the work of other sectors of the criminal justice system and the larger society; and (d) move steadily, as his capacity warrants and opportunity exists, into leadership and executive roles.

The university can play a significant role in broadening the skills of persons already employed by providing an exposure to content beyond the mechanics of agency rules and practice.[4] Since, characteristically, the executive and managerial complement of parole agencies tends to be small, such programs within the state would be of an individualized nature. This, of course, argues for regional, or even national executive and managerial development programs for the parole field.[5]

---

[4]There are a number of excellent sources which relate to executive development courses through university auspices. See, for example, Executive development courses in universities, *Studies in Personnel Policy*, No. 142, 1954; Melvin Anshen: Executive development—in-company vs university programs, *Harvard Business Review*, 32:83-91, September-October, 1954. The National Council on Crime and Delinquency has sponsored several probation management institutes. The literature which they have used has been drawn primarily from the industrial sector due to a lack of specific corrections-related executive development materials. This, of course, raises the issue of generic vs specific training, and whether a manager can manage in any setting, given certain managerial skills.

[5]Ideally, such individualization might do a more effective job in identifying specific areas of training need. On the other hand, however, the cost factor, as well as the duplication of effort, is a problem. See Carroll L. Shartle: *Executive Performance and Leadership*. Englewood Cliffs, N.J., Prentice-Hall, p. 86.

Agency Utilization of University Resources

Study data indicated only narrow utilization of university resources as part of the total parole personnel mission. Work study programs and traineeships were reported as being utilized only in several of the larger states. Professors are used in some departments for in-service training and other training activity.

Just as the corrections field looks to the institutions of higher education for its first line of recruitment, it should be abundantly clear that both sectors, the field agency and the educational center, have a joint responsibility to assist in upgrading the quality of service to the correctional client and to the public. In those few instances where joint ventures have been instituted, with the evaluative inputs which were described earlier, beneficial results have been obtained. Universities today are probably less remote than Galvin describes them:

> In general, the university is a formidable institution to be approached by a non-prestigious, non-affluent client such as corrections. This situation is due in part to the university's traditional resistance to any effort to bring a vocational emphasis into undergraduate curriculum building and research, except in the preparation of teachers.[6]

To this point, a variety of potential involvements has been identified for university participation in the educational and training necessities for the administration of criminal justice field. In a number of places the academic community has reached out or responded to corrections. This appears to have come about more often as a result of the special interest and initiative of a particular faculty member. In contrast to over a hundred police science programs at the bachelor's and associate degree levels, the number of programs at the same levels for corrections are minimal.

In some few instances, correctional administrators have been successful in persuading college or university administrations to make provision for corrections-related programs. But, as Galvin points out, the process can be described as "willy-nilly"—partly

---

[6]John J. Galvin: Issues for the Seminar. In *Criminology and Corrections Programs.* Washington, Joint Commission on Correctional Manpower and Training, July, 1968, p. 1. Notable exceptions to this statement include the Southern Illinois University, University of Minneosta, Florida State University, Michigan State University, Ohio State University, and the Pennsylvania State University.

because of the haphazard way in which programs have originated, but also because of the lack of consensus about the education required for correctional work[7]

The Prognosis for Expanded University Involvement

In a survey reported by Morris and Powers of 109 liberal arts institutions in New England, fifty have a single course in criminology, and only twelve have a second course in juvenile delinquency.[8]

In general, similar surveys in the South, West, and East would support the New England conclusion that:

Those who teach liberal arts courses in criminology are not likely to think of corrections as offering a desirable career opportunity for college graduates, or feel that many suitable opportunities are available for their graduates in the correctional field. This is because they lack adequate information and also because, at present, the opportunities are, in fact, relatively few and the ways to utilize them may not be clear.[9]

The issue of liberal arts involvement in the correctional field is best summed up in a Pennsylvania State University conference report:

There is a distinction that could be drawn between knowledge on the one hand, and skill on the other. Many of the academic disciplines (sociology, anthropology, philosophy, etc.) have as their purpose the acquiring of new knowledge—the emphasis is on research. The emphasis of these academic disciplines has never been, and should not be, toward specifically applying this knowledge to help human beings in trouble. We don't find philosophers, historians, or sociologists normally going out to intervene in the problems of people; when they do, they shift out of the role of historian, economist, etc., and they become something else. . . .[10]

---

[7]John Galvin, *op. cit.,* p. 5.

[8]Albert Morris and Edwin Powers: *The Role of New England Colleges and Universities in correctional staff education. Report of the New England Correctional Manpower and Training Project.* Boston, Massachusetts Correctional Association, 1968, p. 50.

[9]*Ibid.,* p. 51. See also Western Interstate Commission for Higher Education: *Undergraduate Education and Manpower Utilization in the Helping Services,* Boulder, Colorado, 1967; Southern Regional Education Board: *Manpower for Correctional Rehabilitation in the South,* Atlanta, 1966; Pennsylvania Council for Correctional Staff Development: *Education for Career Service in the Correctional Field,* (Report of an Institute), University Park, Pa., 1963; Piven and Alcabes: *op. cit.*

[10]*Education for Career Service in the Correctional Field, op. cit.,* p. 25.

Many college courses, other than those in criminology (which generally is offered through the sociology department), provide administrative or professional education with applications in a variety of fields, of which corrections is one. These include public administration, clinical psychology, teaching, counseling, and vocational rehabilitation, among others. In the main, those disciplines are not oriented towards corrections, and most of the students who take them rarely, if ever, think of their application to a career in corrections. More critically, these students are not likely to have supplemented their specializations in the aforementioned fields with even a single course in the criminal justice area.[11]

Universities could help corrections by assisting in research, providing consultation, training professionals, giving guidance in connection with in-service training programs, and bringing different concepts into the correctional field through the different disciplines.[12] Both universities and correctional agencies should have personnel to do these things cooperatively.

Issues Yet to be Resolved

There remains to be resolved a number of critical issues concerned with the role of the university as it relates to education for the correctional field. Assuming that the university does take on responsibility for the development of educational programs related to corrections, under which departmental auspices will the program be offered? A Joint Commission on Correctional Manpower and Training study in 1968 identified seven "host departments" for such programs in terms of content identity.[13] These included criminal justice, criminology, corrections, police science, public administration, social welfare, and sociology. Insofar as organization is concerned, some programs are located in separate colleges or schools, special centers, departments and divisions, but most are within departments of colleges of liberal arts or are themselves

---

[11]Morris and Powers, *op. cit.*, p. 51.

[12]Manpower for correctional rehabilitation in the south (Report of an Institute). In *Strategies for Meeting Correctional Training and Manpower Needs.* Washington, U.S. Dept. of Justice, Office of Law Enforcement Assistance, 1966.

[13]Loren Karacki and John J. Galvin: Higher education programs in criminology and corrections. In *Criminology and Corrections Programs.* Washington, Joint Commission on Correctional Manpower and Training, 1968, pp. 14-15.

separate departments. It is reasonable to assume that differences in auspices will be reflected in differing kinds of course offerings.

A second set of issues relates to the level of education involved, since current programs range from the predegree (i.e. certificate), associate, bachelor, master, to doctoral levels. Programs can be identified as available at each level, although their numbers are not substantial. Table XX presents the most recent data on established curricula.

Table XX delineates between "established" and "new" programs. The former refers to those offering a formally approved specialization or degree in criminology or corrections, which by 1967-68 had been in existence long enough to have graduated students. New programs differed only in terms of the time of their establishment.

Karacki and Galvin indicate that established programs in sociology departments more generally offer specialization rather than special degrees, while in the overwhelming majority (ten out of twelve) established programs in criminology and corrections offered special degrees.[14] Of some significance, and perhaps providing an indication of a trend, is that five of the ten new programs were outside traditional sociology and political science departments. Since the numbers we are dealing with are small, it is still too early to detect whether this reflects the pattern suggested by Piven and Alcabes for the development of new institutional resources for training and research in criminal justice.[15]

Programs which offer the bachelor's or master's degrees are engaged in preparing persons to work in the corrections area, either in the institutional or field services at the adult or juvenile levels. On the other hand, the doctoral level program is more likely to de-emphasize corrections, seeing it as a segment of the total criminal justice system, and with primary emphasis on the research area, development of college level teachers, and publication of criminological literature.

It is for the universities to decide how educational programs for the correctional area will be provided. Specification of curriculum, degree requirements, and the like are within the preroga-

---

[14]Karacki and Galvin, *ibid.,* p. 13.

[15]Piven and Alcabes, *op. cit.,* p. 37, *et seq.*

TABLE XX
TYPE OF AWARDS GRANTED IN PROGRAMS OF CRIMINOLOGY AND CORRECTIONS BY PROGRAM STATUS AND DEPARTMENT (ACADEMIC YEAR 1967-68)

Program Status and Department	Number of Schools	None or Unknown	Undergraduate Only				Undergraduate and Graduate Programs							Graduate Only	
			S	B	C and B	C	C and M	S and M	B and M	C,B and M	S,M and D	B,M and D	C,B, M and D	M and D	D
Total	63	21	8	4	1	12	1	3	3	2	1	3	1	1	2
Established	33	....	5	3	..	12	1	2	2	2	1	3	1	1	..
Criminology	4	....	..	1	..	....	..	..	1	..	..	1	1	..	..
Sociology	21	....	4	..	..	11	..	2	..	1	..	2	..	1	..
Other	8	....	1	2	..	1	1	..	1	1	1	..	..	..	..
New	10	1	3	1	1	....	..	1	1	..	•	..	..	..	2
Nondegree	20	20	..	..	..	....	..	..	..	..	..	..	..	..	..

Key: S = Specialization
    B = Bachelor's
    C = Certificate (for nondegree students)
    M = Master's
    D = Doctor's

Source: Adapted from staff documents, provided by Dr. B. Frank of the Joint Commission on Correctional Manpower and Training.

tive of the educational establishment. But there needs to be a relevance between the educational program and the entry position for the graduate, and this calls for close interaction between the university and the field.

In view of the critical shortage of educators with first hand knowledge of the internal workings of the criminal justice system, it is urgent that a viable mechanism be developed which would exchange experienced practitioners without the requisite academic credentials for credentialled educators without practical field experience. Other possibilities include the development of joint appointments.

Conclusion

In this chapter, several dimensions related to education for the field of corrections have been considered. It can be concluded that education for corrections can be located as a discrete educational area, rather than as a sector of sociology, law, psychology, psychiatry, or social work, governed exclusively by the educational models and principles generic to those fields. Admittedly, corrections is subsumed within the broader field of the human welfare services which also include education, medicine, law, and religion, all of which are directed to meet the needs of designated groups within society. Further, as a field of practice for people with various professional skills, corrections is a consumer of the products of a number of disciplines and occupational groups which constitute its working parts. But corrections, in this view, has a unique content as a professional area and, moreover, it contributes its own unique knowledge to the basic disciplines.[16]

---

[16]Charles L. Newman: Educational issues and strategies for the field of corrections. *The Quarterly* (The Pennsylvania Association on Probation, Parole, and Corrections), *24*:18, Spring, 1967.

Chapter VII

Employment Conditions In Adult Parole

IN THE COURSE OF THIS STUDY, evidence has been accumulated which supports the contention that wide variations exist in the United States relative to personnel practices. The previous chapter provided a model wherein the correctional field, as a totality, could benefit from an interrelationship with the university sector which could provide educationally prepared individuals.

It should be apparent, however, that no matter how well prepared the individual is when he is employed, unless the climate in which he works is appropriate, he will not remain with the agency. These include the availability of adequate secretarial help to handle the volume of paper work, which is an ever-present part of the parole task, and suitable office and desk space to carry out interviews and related work. Most importantly, the agency must have a well-defined policy manual which spells out, not only in terms of ideals, but in positive direction, what it is that the agency is attempting to do and the means by which it wants to accomplish those ends. The agency must provide the incentives, both financial and psychological, which will challenge the worker to perform in a professional manner as he has been trained to do.

Critically, the parole field position cannot be a dead end. The agency must structure opportunities for promotion so that individuals with the capacity can move into more responsible positions in the overall structure.

Promotion Policy

Whether an agency should adopt a formal promotion program is often a perplexing issue for personnel officials to determine. And if the decision is in the affirmative, there is still the difficult task of establishing formal promotion methods. Legal provisions, civil service rules, customs, local personalities, and other factors may affect the formulation of promotional plans.

In reviewing the arguments for and against a promotional plan, Torpey suggests a number of principles which appear to have applicability to the parole field.[1] Among these are included the suggestion that the initial competitive area should be the organizational unit in which the employee works.[2] Promotion standards should be fairly and uniformly applied. The plan should be committed to writing and disseminated among all employees.[3] During the formulation of a plan, opportunity should be afforded to employees to criticize, comment, and make recommendations. Finally, periodic evaluation should be made of the effectiveness of the promotion program.

Three options are available generally to agencies in regard to candidacy for promotional positions. These are (a) all positions are promotional within the agency, and not open to outside competition; (b) all positions are open-competitive, without a residence requirement; or (c) all positions are open-competitive, but with a residence requirement.

In general, most jurisdictions (52.5%) recognize the morale advantage of a policy which fills vacancies by internal promotion. More commonly small agencies maintain an open policy for promotion, either with (3) or without (9) residence requirements. On the other hand, large states predominantly allow for promotional opportunities exclusively within the agency (10). No significant trend was established for middle-sized agencies, which more commonly limited promotions to within the agency (5) compared to the open policy (3).

There are, of course, dangers inherent in both promotional plans. A closed system engenders the possibility of stagnation.[4] That is to say, through the process of inbreeding, the agency may

[1]William G. Torpey: Promotion from Within. *Public Personnel Review, 13*:176-178, October, 1952.

[2]*Ibid.*, p. 178.

[3]*Ibid.*

[4]Felix A. Nigro: *Public Administration Readings and Documents.* New York, Rinehart, 1951, p. 278.

lose some of its vitality, since new ideas are not infused into the agency. Even with a promotion-from-within policy, the defects can be mitigated with a well-developed and meaningful training program. Procedures can be developed which induce staff to participate in educational programs, attain advanced degrees, and attend state, regional, and national conferences in order to gain new points of view.

The findings to the question are stated in Table XXI.

TABLE XXI
POLICY REGARDING PROMOTIONAL OPPORTUNITY   (N=40)

	Small	Intermediate	Large
Open, no residence	19.5%	7.5%	7.5%
Open, residence	7.5%	0.0%	2.5%
Closed, promotional	15.0%	12.5%	25.0%

**Participation in Outside
Training Opportunitites**

One measure of the extent to which such attempts to remedy the limits of a closed system can be found in the stated policy regarding field staff participation in national, regional, and state professional meetings at agency expense. Twelve of the seventeen responding small states permitted conference participation. Large states more commonly did not permit field staff to attend conferences at agency expense (six of thirteen). Obviously cost is a factor when the number of possible participants extends into the hundreds. Interestingly, intermediate states more commonly did permit such participation, though generally this was limited to the state level conference.

Most states indicated that permission to attend conferences was predicated upon the availability of budgeted funds, as well as the geographic location of the meetings. In all classifications, attendance at state meetings is more commonly permitted than at regional or national ones.

In view of the penurious nature of the correctional budget, we can speculate that opportunities for the infusion of new ideas through the conference route is extremely limited.

Significantly, only half of the states permitting state conference attendance allowed for national meeting participation, though by and large national meetings generally represent a higher quality of program than can be found at the state level. Distributions are presented in Table XXII.

TABLE XXII
FIELD STAFF PARTICIPATION AT CONFERENCES   (N=40)

	Small	Intermediate	Large
State meetings	30.0%	15.0%	15.0%
Regional meetings	25.0%	10.0%	12.5%
National meetings	12.5%	7.5%	10.0%

The advantages of an open promotional system suggest a greater flexibility on the part of the agency to meet its managerial and administrative needs. The problem of morale, which it engenders, is a significant one to be reckoned with, however. The resolution appears to be found in Nigro's statement: "It would seem that a desirable general policy would be that promotion is to be the preferred method only when the qualifications of persons available for promotion are at least equal to those of persons available for transfer, reinstatement, or selection from an open competitive register."[5]

Administrative Level Positions

Entry into administrative level positions is by two routes: promotion and appointment. There is no consistent pattern utilized by parole agencies. In small departments, there is an even division of both patterns, and in several states both procedures are used. A wide variety of individuals is involved in various states related to appointment of administrative officers. In some instances, the appointment of the parole executive is by the Parole Board; the director of the larger department of which the parole agency is a division; by the political executive; or some special board related to the political sector. The preponderance of large agencies (91%) promotes administrative officials, while intermediate agencies use the appointive approach in 75 percent of the cases.

The fundamental factor contributing to the success or failure

---

[5]Nigro: *ibid.*, p. 279. California reports an interdepartmental promotional scheme.

of both promotional and appointive processes relates to the supply of qualified candidates. A successful promotion system anticipates a constant induction of competent and qualified individuals who will at some later point become eligible for upward movement within the system. A successful appointive system anticipates experienced correctional administrators available outside the correctional system. Since neither case appears to prevail, it is extremely difficult to rate one system over the other as it presently exists.

Service Rating Systems

Whether or not an agency utilizes an internal promotional system for moving personnel into supervisory, managerial, or administrative positions, it is critical that some scheme be utilized in order to evaluate staff performance. The effective management and evaluation of personnel should involve day-to-day contact between executive, supervisor, and staff. The nature of the parole job, the dispersed distribution of facilities with small personnel complements, and the decentralization of operations all serve to complicate the evaluative process of parole personnel.

In order to plan for staff management and development, it is vital to know how well people do their jobs.[6] Equally critical is a shared understanding of what the job actually entails. Unfortunately, as in many of the human service areas, the job is described in terms of client needs, rather than agent performance. The techniques for implementing these goals remain to be developed.

Klein, in describing the elements necessary for workable service ratings, includes (a) a workable system of recording fact and opinion on quantity and quality of performance, and (b) thorough understanding by those who do the rating of the objectives and problems in using such a system.[7]

---

[6]A significant difficulty in evaluating the quality of personnel performance rests in the vagueness of the job itself. As one respondent indicated: "This matter of evaluating staff is a concern of ours. It is hard to determine whether or not a Parole Officer is doing an efficient job. He could be well liked by officials and his supervisor, dress neatly, write a very good report and still be doing a lousy job. Criteria of measurement for efficiency in individuals working with people is hard to come by." Questionnaire response from Gail D. Hughes, Chief State Supervisor, Missouri Board of Probation and Parole.

[7]Alice Campbell Klein: *Civil Service in Public Welfare.* New York, Russell Sage Foundation, 1940, p. 192.

All of the intermediate and large agencies indicated the utilization of some sort of service rating system. To a lesser extent (64%) small states indicate the use of service ratings. Wide variations exist, however, with reference to the frequency of such evaluation, as is shown in Table XXIII.

TABLE XXIII
FREQUENCY OF SERVICE RATING   (N=40)

	Small	Intermediate	Large
Quarterly	5%	13%	8%
Semiannually	28%	37%	22%
Annually	44%	50%	70%
No Rating	23%	....	....

What happens to people who do not perform up to expectation, whatever that standard may be, was another subject for inquiry. In the main, responses indicated almost universally that normative deprivations and sanctions were imposed. That is to say, formal or informal talks are held with the staff person, overt or subtle warnings are given, and generally the opportunity to "improve" is provided. In some instances reports of remunerative deprivation, i.e. the withholding of a pay increase, may be invoked. In the main, however, this study found that sanctions to the point of dismissal are rarely invoked. For example, in 1967, small agencies discharged a total of three parole personnel for cause, and four in 1968. Fourteen small agencies indicated no discharges for cause in either year.[8]

With a substantially larger personnel base from which to draw, the intermediate agencies, similarly, did not discharge personnel for cause. In 1967, nationally, five persons were dismissed; in 1968, the number was seven. Half of the intermediate size departments had no dismissals at all. The pattern continues to the largest departments, where in 1967, seventeen persons were discharged and eighteen the following year. In both 1967 and 1968, among the largest agencies, four departments did not discharge anyone.

---

[8]One state, Mississippi, indicated three discharges for political reasons in 1967. Broadly speaking, this might be considered cause based on the lack of good judgment by the persons concerned to support the "right" candidate.

A variety of explanations can be developed for the low rate of dismissal:

1. Agencies, in the selective process, do so superior a job that dismissals are rarely necessary.
2. Persons who are unsuited to the work choose to resign before they are dismissed.
3. The resignation route is encouraged by administration, rather than dismissal.
4. Lacking standards, agencies do not eliminate personnel, since any work done is better than none.
5. Dismissal procedures are so complex as to make firing a difficult process for the agency administrator.

These points are discussed singly below.

1. There is, of course, no evidence to substantiate the notion that agencies do a superior selection job. If, in fact, Piven and Alcabes are correct in their statement that parole executives prefer and seek personnel with a master's degree in social work in order to perform the job expectation, then every agency in the United States is settling for considerably less than the desired norm.[9] Data from this study found that no agency requires a master's degree,[10] a majority prefer a bachelor's degree without specification as to area of academic preparation (70%), but almost half provide for substitution of "experience" for academic preparation.

2. It is reasonable to accept the notion that personnel, discovering that they are unsuited to the parole task, leave the agency voluntarily; and no doubt this occurs in some instances. In a recent Missouri study reported by Hughes, lack of interest or ability occurred in only 7 percent of the instances where resignations occurred.[11]

---

[9]Piven and Alcabes: *op. cit.*, p. 11. According to an NCCD (1967) study reported by them, no adult parole agencies had agents with graduate social work degrees.

[10]Minnesota currently requires a bachelor's degree for entry position; however, current policy urges the acquisition of a social work degree at the master's level. T. F. Spencer, Personnel Director, reports that, "Requiring MSW has caused insecurity in B.A. staff and heightened tension activity." Questionnaire response.

[11]Gail D. Hughes, Chief State Supervisor, Missouri Board of Probation and Parole. Response to questionnaire item. Other reasons given included: salaries (79%), lack of promotional opportunities (20%), agency policy (11%), poor supervision (10%), caseloads (7%). These findings seem to support other informal studies, except for the problem related to salary, which may be the *easy* excuse in this case.

3. There is some similarity between this option and the preceding one. The principal difference relates to the perceptiveness of the employee in determining his own unsuitability. Again, solid evidence to support the contention that administrators encourage resignation rather than have to dismiss is lacking, but it is reasonable to assume that such practices do exist.

4. There is ample evidence that the performance of the parole officer function is difficult to evaluate. Operating almost entirely as an independent agent, it is virtually impossible to measure the quality of performance, except in terms of written records, which may or may not reflect the quality of the job being done. The quality of the caseload itself, the severity of the problems experienced by the correctional client, the factors related to community acceptance or rejection of the parolee, family relationships, and a host of other factors, all serve to complicate the success of the agent's work mission. The evaluation cannot be gauged in terms of successful completions of parole, numbers of revocations, or even the number of visits made, since the quality of the visit is virtually impossible to quantify. Thus, it is not unlikely that agencies, while striving to accomplish high level performances, are frequently satisfied if minimal measurable expectations are fulfilled. These would include reasonable congeniality, a coherence in report writing, and a fairly regular attendance to the work of the agency. In the absence of well defined performance criteria, agencies cannot be held in contempt for following such a course of action.

5. There is evidence to support the idea that once a person is hired, and successfully passes through the probationary appointment period, he is most difficult to remove from the parole service. Significantly, this problem is not unique to the correctional area, but pervades the public service generally. Moreover, it can be anticipated that as changes in the public employer-employee relations occur, with collective bargaining emerging as a right in the public as in the private sector, we can anticipate an ever-increasing reluctance on the part of administrators to discharge for cause, unless the conditions are so blatant as to cry for action.[12] In actual

---

[12]Howard J. Anderson (Ed.): *Public Employee Organization and Bargaining.* (A Report on the Joint Conference of the Association of Labor Mediator Agencies and The National Association of State Labor Relations Agencies, August 19 to August 24, 1968) Washington, The Bureau of National Affairs, Inc., 1968, pp. 1-13.

practice, the complexity of the process is described by one respondent to the study:

> Formal rating of unsatisfactory must be first approved in Central Office and a detailed form is prepared. Employee has appeal rights. These ratings are rarely given due to the complications that ensue. An employee appraisal system is also used annually to provide a means for the employee and supervisor to review together in a formal way the employee's good and bad points. Both the ratings and appraisal are required by the state government and neither work too well.[13]

Conditions of Employment

Related to the matter of effective job performance is the constellation of factors which have been broadly defined as human relations factors in personnel administration.

Effective personnel administration seeks to provide those conditions of employment "which enable employees to achieve as many as possible of their individual and group goals and aspirations and, at the same time, they are encouraged and motivated to give their best efforts to the organization in achieving its objectives."[14] There is no question of the fact that dissatisfied or aggrieved employees are not willing or enthusiastic workers.[15]

Morse reports a study conducted at the University of Michigan Survey Research Center which attempted to measure intrinsic job satisfaction. The findings, while not specifically related to parole, offer certain conclusions which may be valuable to the parole administrator.[16] To the questions, "How well do you like the sort of work you are doing?" and "Do you get any feeling of accom-

---

[13]Questionnaire response from Henry B. Bankhead, Associate Personnel Administrator, New York State Division of Parole.

[14]Charles A. Meyers: "Basic employment relations. In Arthur Kornhauser, Robert Dubin, and Arthur M. Ross (Eds.): *Industrial Conflict*. New York, McGraw-Hill, 1954, p. 319.

[15]Evidence of the relationship between enterprise objectives and the reduction of conflict in employer-employee relations may be found in the work of the social psychologists on leadership. N. C. Morse: *Employee Satisfaction, Supervision, and Morale in an Office Situation*. University of Michigan, Survey Research Center Report, 1953.

[16]Morse: *ibid.*, as cited in Daniel Katz: Satisfactions and deprivations in industrial life. In Arthur Kornhauser, *et. al.*, *op. cit.*, pp. 91-93.

plishment from the work you are doing?" the results strongly suggested that:

> . . . greater gratifications found by higher-level occupational groups are not wholly a function of wages and conditions of work. People do derive important satisfactions in the expression of their skills, in interesting and challenging work, and in the sense of accomplishment from successful performance.[17]

In the same study, it was also found that employees who evidenced higher intrinsic job satisfaction tended to be people who described their jobs as having variety and as giving them some chance to make decisions.[18]

It appears that the opportunity to participate in the decision-making process, i.e. the opportunity for self-determination, is an important variable in job satisfaction and, ultimately, in morale. This is not to suggest that the field officer should make all the decisions by himself. That process is included in the supervisory and administrative responsibility. But, as we can assume frequently happens, the parole officer can find himself thinking of the decision-making group as "they," either identifying himself with the client, or at least blocked in communication with administration.

The converse to the denial of decision-making prerogatives by lower-level staff is equally dangerous. The nature of parole work, with its regional offices throughout a state, permits the staff members to operate autonomously to a high degree. Such a situation may contribute to the parole officer's isolation from administrative direction and policy. It is not unlikely that, given the circumstances of relative autonomy and distance from the center of policy formulation, the field worker may usurp the policy-making role and tend to oppose himself to the constituted policy-making group.

This whole question is, of course, one fraught with importance for the parole field and remains unanswered at this juncture. Further research is certainly necessary to test out the hypothesis as stated above, and the conclusions reached upon the basis of sound empirical research should have major significance for the administration of parole.

---

[17]Morse: *ibid.*, p. 92.
[18]*Ibid.*

The ingredients which go into the making of morale are far beyond the scope of this study and would involve a treatise by itself.

Part of the parole employee's feeling about his job can be related to salary satisfaction. Where the individual is highly motivated and interested in the work of the parole field, and where circumstances preclude his moving to another geographic area where better salaries are offered, the dilemma is resolved by the manifested dissatisfaction, either implicit or explicit, against the "administration," the legislature, or the generalized "they." Again, the roots of this problem lie in faulty lines of communication.

Where channels of communication between staff and line employees are so diffuse as to obscure the dissemination of information, the latter group may gather the feeling that administration is feathering its own nest, to the sacrifice of the lower echelons. Communication must also work upward in the opportunity for lower echelon employees to communicate grievances, real or imagined, so that they can be resolved. Good working relationships derive from a number of sources. Attitudes of administrative officials toward employee groups, and policies in regard to promotion, transfer, or demotion, produce employee satisfaction commensurate with the energy entailed. Effective leadership may compensate for working conditions or policies which might otherwise depress morale considerably.[19]

Establishing Communications

In order that the parole agency may administer its program effectively, its organization must provide for channels through which communications may flow. Through these channels should flow a two-way stream of ideas and operations. As the transfer of meaning, communication is the fundamental aspect of interdependence among human beings. Without communication, it would be impossible to transfer the repository of experience from the line to staff levels, both horizontally and vertically.

As obvious as it may seem as to both the necessity and de-

---

[19]Civil Service Assembly Committee Reports: *Employee Relations in the Public Service,* Chicago, 1942; and *Placement and Probation in the Public Service,* Chicago, 1946; *op. cit.*

sirability of establishing effective patterns of communication within an agency and between administrative and field levels, such patterns are not often constructively established. The evidence from experimental social psychology supports the conclusion that the greater the isolation, the more idiosyncratic the pattern of operation. Conversely, the more frequent the meetings and interchange among members of different groups, the more similar are the ways of acting in the groups concerned. This is particularly relevant where staff is widely dispersed across a state, and where cultural differences exist as a consequence of intrastate regional variations.

Methods of Internal Staff Communications

The major contribution to the growth and development of workers is made as they are encouraged to fully use their knowledge, skills, and experience to further the aims of the agency. In order that he may perform at maximum capacity, the staff member must develop both a sense of identification with that agency purpose and philosophy, and a feeling that he is an important part of the total administration. In such a climate the worker is stimulated to seek new knowledge and develop skills for more effective performance.

As was pointed out earlier, communication plays an important role in the development of sound agency administration and practice. As Tebow has stated:

> Unless the information channels are lubricated with understanding of agency purpose and plans, staff members may direct their energy to keeping well-watered the "grape-vine" from which a certain amount of information (or misinformation) will spread. Information obtained by this means, rather than by planned sharing, frequently results in unnecessary staff interpretation, dissatisfaction, and resentments.[20]

Administrative Leadership

Only a word can be said here regarding the relationship of leadership to the parole administrator, since full discussion of this point would also involve discussion of the administrator's place

---

[20]Hilda P. Tebow: *Staff Development As An Integral Part of Administration.* Public Assistance Report No. 35. Washington, Government Printing Office, 1959, p. 1.

in the whole administrative process. There is a general agreement that the most important and most difficult task of an agency administrator is leadership, not command. This leadership has as its goal the development of the desire and will to work together for a common purpose on the part of all staff. Such leadership calls for initiative in direction and the ability to coordinate ideas and efforts throughout the whole agency. But, as Mary Follett has so ably presented the idea, coordination is not a culminating process.

> You cannot always bring together the *results* of departmental activities and expect to coordinate them. You must have an organization which will permit inter-weaving all along the line. Strand should weave with strand, and then we shall not have the clumsy task of trying to patch together finished webs.[21]

Such leadership functions can be carried out to an appropriate degree only if communication channels are open for the free flow of information. If top agency administration is disorganized, uncoordinated, and cloudy as to purpose and function, then the best efforts of operating staff can be met only with blocking and frustration.

Grievance Procedure

For the greatest effectiveness in identifying and modifying the problems which are encountered in the day-to-day performance of the job, it is vital that staff be given the opportunity for conferences with supervisory and administrative personnel. Moreover, any good system of administration must include a plan whereby the employee can appeal personnel decisions against him if he feels strongly about them. While in a previous era, we might have been satisfied to suggest that if an employee were dissatisfied he could leave the agency employ; today our concept of fair play rejects such a notion. In the Hughes study cited earlier, dissatisfaction with agency policy and poor supervision were designated as the basis for employee separation.[22] It is equally important that agencies

---

[21]Mary Follett: *The Illusion of Final Authority*. A paper presented at the meeting of the "Taylor Society" (now the Society for the Advancement of Management) in New York, December, 1926, 7 pp. Reproduced by Bureau of Employment Security, Federal Security Agency, March, 1941.

[22]Hughes: *op. cit.*, Note 11 supra.

establish machinery for impartial review of supervisors' actions and judgments.[23]

Employee and Fringe Benefits

Finally, we come to consider these provisions which relate to benefits which agencies provide in addition to compensation. This study did not attempt to compile salary data, because of its volatile quality and the difficulty which emerges in attempting to assess meaning to the data. All states except one reported a range of salaries within a particular grade. When the agency maintains such a range within any particular grade, and has the authority to appoint at above the minimum, it is reasonable to asume that in a tight manpower situation the practice will differ from those of a favorable personnel situation. Similarly, when salary increases are based on merit, it is virtually impossible to tell how many people are at what stage of salary development. Even though the data was not collected, we can speculate with a high degree of accuracy that all kinds of inconsistencies would show up between small, intermediate, and large departments based on regional variations, qualifications sought, general economy of the state, and a variety of other factors.

A relatively similar pattern was discovered between the various sized agencies as to the use of merit pay increases as opposed to those on an automatic basis. The distribution favored merit pay increases by only 9 percent, or a difference of four states.

Similar problems emerge in relation to the evaluation of fringe benefits which are available to the staff member. The definition of "fringe" is patterned after Belcher's typology, and includes (a) extra payments for time worked, (b) payments for time not worked, (c) payments for employment security, and (d) payments for employee services.[24]

Extra Payment for Time Worked

The nature of the parole job is such that officers, supervisors,

---

[23]*Cf.*, Harry L. Case: *Personnel Policy in A Public Agency* New York, Harper, 1955, pp. 66-67. According to Case, the existence of grievance machinery provides for striking a balance in the authority of the supervisor, giving him enough support in his decisions, so that he can control his organization and yet subject to overruling on his mistakes.

[24]David W. Belcher: *Wage and Salary Administration*. Englewood Cliffs, N. J., Prentice-Hall, 1959, p. 454 *et seq.*

and administrators commonly work hours that extend beyond the customary work week. This is especially true for field officers who may have to spend evenings and weekends either conducting investigations or maintaining client contact in the field, since those are the only times when the parolee may be available. An examination of agency practice revealed three variations of practice: compensatory time off, overtime pay, and no provision for time or financial reimbursement. Marked variations were found both within states for the several classes of employees (administrators, supervisors, field personnel) and between the various agencies.

At the administrative level, only one jurisdiction (the District of Columbia) provided for overtime compensation. Almost half of the jurisdiction had no provision in their policy to compensate administrative overtime. A slight increase favoring compensatory time off for supervisors was reflected in the addition of three states allowing time payment. A significant increase was noted at the field level, particularly in the large agencies, which almost universally (92%) permitted compensatory time off. The distributions are shown in Table XXIV.

TABLE XXIV
AGENCY POLICY FOR OVERTIME WORK

	Compensatory Time Off			Overtime Compensation			No Provision		
	S.	I.	L.	S.	I.	L.	S.	I.	L.
Administrators	7	5	8	1	0	0	10	3	6
Supervisors	8	6	10	1	0	0	9	2	4
Field agents	9	6	13	1	0	0	8	2	1

Key: S=small, I=intermediate, L=large.

Payment for Time Not Worked

While government provisions for vacation and leaves may not, in many instances, be so liberal or so flexible as those in private industry, a pattern was detected which suggested that increasing rewards for long tenure were being provided in a number of states. The minimum number of allowed vacation days reported was one per month. In most instances the number was augmented by a quarter to a half day per month after the employee had worked for the agency beyond five or ten years.

Similar patterns exist in relation to sick leave. Ordinarily, a minimum base is established, beyond which the staff person can accumulate additional credits, generally up to some maximum limit. Additionally, because of the sometimes hazardous nature of the parole officer job, special provisions are made for injuries sustained in line of duty. There is no common pattern, with alternatives ranging from Workman's Compensation to early retirement with disability provisions.

Payment for Employee Security

All reporting agencies except Hawaii indicated the participation of employees in a state-maintained or supported retirement program. Wide variations, however, exist with reference to the extent of employee contributions, the base coverage, the years of service required for eligibility, and the participation of the state agency in the plan. In some instances, the retirement program is augmented by the employee participation in the federal social security program. Questionnaire results were not of sufficient quality in this area to warrant reporting.

Payment for Employee Services

The nature of the parole job is such that transportation is frequently necessary for the performance of duties. Two general patterns of agency policy have emerged from the study data: (a) the employee operates his own car, with either a fixed monthly allowance for use, or mileage repayment for actual utilization; (b) the employee operates a state vehicle.

In about half of the jurisdictions, both plans are utilized. Reimbursement rates vary widely from a reported minimum of seven cents a mile to a maximum of twelve cents. Three states reported allowing a fixed monthly rate for the use of the employee's car, but did not specify the amount.

It should be reasonably apparent that the intent of having employees out in the field is seriously jeopardized if the expense of his travel will have to be augmented from his own earnings. There is no reasonable basis for the wide disparity between the lowest and the highest reimbursing agencies, since fuel, vehicle, and maintenance costs are relatively equal across the country. If the position calls for travel, then the agency should provide the vehicle. This would remove the burden from the employee to maintain a work vehicle, and certainly encourage him to spend more time in the field when the job requires it, without the problem of having to subsidize the agency for his work.

A variety of other fringe benefits are beginning to emerge in the public service. These include such items as salary continuation during educational leave, tuition subsidy, conference expense reimbursement, and the like. In general the data collected from the study was too incomplete to draw any final conclusions for the parole field. If, however, the path which has been blazed in the public welfare and mental health areas becomes characteristic for parole, we can anticipate an increasing amount of benefit to accrue to staff in order to attain educational and training objectives, ultimately to the benefit of the employing agency.

Chapter VIII
Summary and Conclusions

THE ORGANIZATION OF A PAROLE AGENCY, its location within the structure of government, policy formulations, management, fiscal control, program planning, and analysis are all vital ingredients in its administration, but none of the foregoing is more essential than competent personnel. The history of public administration, as Nigro points out, is littered with the wreckage of well-planned organizational structures because of inadequately trained or inefficient personnel.[1]

The correctional field has long known the dearth of trained workers, and the difficulty faced from time to time both in retaining those who are competent, and in the replacement of capable persons to fill vacancies.

Part of the difficulty, we have seen, rests with the inadequacy of definition of the parole task itself. Much of the job specification of the parole officer is defined in terms of community objectives; namely, protection of society and the restoration of the offender to a law abiding status. By and large, the nature of the job itself has been ignored, except to classify it as one of the various occupations within the human services sector requiring a certain knowledge base, and specifying certain experience qualities as desirable. Unfortunately, however, learning about behavioral mechanisms and social systems does not provide the parole officer with the skill and techniques necessary to modify behavior. Moreover, since the objectives are defined in such lofty terms as resocialization, rehabilitation, and social adjustment, the specifications are extremely difficult to define.

---

[1]Felix A. Nigro: *Public Administration Readings and Documents.* New York, Rinehart, 1951, p. 201.

Aside from the crucial aspect of weeding out the misfits, the more positive consideration of who should be selected to work in parole services presents a dilemma of much broader dimensions.

Although the literature abounds with opinions as to the type of person who should be employed as a parole officer, hiring standards indicate that such persons are rarely employed. In part, this is due to the fact that persons with professional training beyond the bachelor's degree rarely, if ever, seek employment in the corrections field at the adult level. The very nature of the standards themselves for employment, the low salaries, and the fact that the majority of persons already employed and doing the job are of lesser educational preparation, serve to discourage the entry of more highly educated persons into parole work. More importantly, however, there has been no evidence produced which would support the contention that individuals prepared at the master's level in social work, or any of the other clinical areas, do a more effective job by any standard of measure which one might choose to define. Thus, before we can seek to alter the educational standard for entry into the parole field, it becomes critical to define the nature of the parole job in terms of concrete examples of the activities to be performed and the type of knowledge and skill necessary to carry out those activities. Simply stated, unless we know what it is the parole agent does, it is not possible to know how he should be trained and educated to do the job.

Wide variations were found to exist in relation to recruitment, selection, and employee benefit factors. Induction training, as well as ongoing in-service training and staff development, varies widely both in quality, quantity, and structure throughout the country.

Promotional opportunities, moving up in the system, also vary from state to state. Some systems are closed; others are open. Generally, experience, rather than educational achievement, is mandated, leading to problems of supervision and administration, for what is required to be a good caseworker at the field level is different from the capacity to manage or administer. In closed systems the possibility of lateral entry is immediately excluded; thus, on the one hand, a career system is maintained, but on the other hand, new ideas, systems, and techniques are excluded.

The smallness, even in the largest agencies, of the personnel complement seriously handicaps opportunities for upward mobility within the system, and many agencies reported that the lack of promotional opportunity (which is related in part to salary) is a significant cause of staff turnover.

In spite of the availability of massive infusions of federal funds to the criminal justice area, the federal largess has not yet been felt in the correctional field, and more particularly in parole. Notwithstanding the problems elaborated upon above in relation to the nature of education and training, the availability of federal funds should provide an increasing opportunity for persons both in the field and outside of it to become increasingly exposed to academic experience.

Probably the most difficult problem yet to be faced by the criminal justice field, and parole in particular, is the lack of any real cohesiveness as to intent and objective as reflected by a common lack of leadership from within the field or direction by professional organizations outside of it. For the most part, the two national professional organizations, The National Council on Crime and Delinquency and The American Correctional Association, have been unable to engender an acceptance of their leadership role. Universities, in their traditional noninvolvement role, have failed to recognize both the significance of the personnel problem in the administration of criminal justice and in their responsibility to accept a team role in defining directions or objectives, as they have in other professional areas such as medicine, law, and engineering.

While the principle objective of this study was to examine personnel practice in adult parole systems, it was necessary to seek out the administrative structures in which the parole task is performed. The conclusion, though not startling to the student of the field, is that wide variations in the administrative placement of parole services exist, and that these diverse administrative arrangements unquestionably create wide variations in which the parole agent task is performed.

Effective administration results primarily from a constructive, efficient approach in the handling of the job between the organizational unit and the individual employee who shares in that joint responsibility. Requisite, then, is the development of policy, procedure, and activity aimed at the achievement of a common program purpose. In some states, positive movement in that direction can be identified, but in the main, progress is very slow. It is difficult to identify a common philosophy, no less a common set of practices across the country.

Ideally, agencies should be moving toward the development of an agency climate in which individuals are stimulated to seek the knowledge and skills necessary to high level performance, and to be creative. This requires that the agency can identify with clarity its program purposes and scope of services to be provided. It should be apparent that the definition of the nature of services has a direct bearing on the type of personnel who must be retained to carry out those services.

Job descriptions, where they exist, tend to be stated in the most general terms. There needs to be developed in virtually every parole jurisdiction, a clearly-stated, current job description for each level of parole officer position, indicating the scope of responsibility, authority, and the level of performance which is expected.

Closely tied to the need for appropriate job descriptions is the critical necessity for the development of career ladders and lateral entry and movement across the field. There is an urgent need to formulate models wherein individuals who remain with a system in case management roles can continue to receive financial rewards without the necessity of moving into managerial or administrative posts for which they may neither be interested nor qualified. Equally important is that the correctional field must begin to shed its parochial attachments in terms of recruiting, and its discriminatory practices in relation to the hiring of women, former offenders, and minority group members.

This study identified a critical need for training resources, both in terms of personnel and the development of sound induction training strategies, and in-service training programs. Related to upgrading the educational qualifications of incumbent staff, it is urgent that agencies begin to identify appropriate courses of study, and provide educational leave and stipend help for staff to engage themselves. However, unless the agency is prepared to reward the individual who upgrades his knowledge and skill with work assignments and salary commensurate with his newly developed talents, then the dollar cost of such development will be wasted.

The distribution of educational resources related to the correctional field was found to be uneven. The Piven-Alcabes study and the work of the Joint Commission on Correctional Manpower and Training have reinforced the impression held both in the academic community and in the field that we do not yet know what it is that each expects of the other, in terms of educational preparation and field performance. The model presented for a specialized undergraduate degree appears to present one avenue of approach to the education of personnel for the corrections area. Much more research is needed, however, as to the relevance of that or similar models, as well as the applicability of two-year and certificate programs for identifiable positions within the correctional apparatus.

The paucity of corrections and criminology programs at the doctoral level presents a serious problem in relation to the production of qualified researchers, teachers, and theorists for the criminal justice field. Temporary palliatives, such as exchange of personnel, were recommended as a means of upgrading both the academic programs and the field agency performance.

It is abundantly clear that massive infusions of money are necessary in the parole field to add necessary personnel, upgrade salaries, and to provide the necessary ancillary services and facilities to get the work done.

Finally, responsible administration must take on the responsibility for having its program operations evaluated to determine the extent of progress toward stated goals and objectives. Such an examination produces facts that serve as a basis for accounting for agency activities and for planning changes when they are needed to improve the agency's program. With that information in hand, the agency can then move toward future personnel planning, through retraining of existing staff when that is necessary, and the addition of staff with skills appropriate to its newly identified program objectives.

Appendix A

Agencies Replying to the Study Questionnaire

Small Departments (under fifty supervisors, field, and institutional parole officers)

Alaska	Mississippi	(18)
Connecticut	Montana	
District of Columbia	Nevada	
Hawaii	New Mexico	
Idaho	North Dakota	
Iowa	South Dakota	
Kansas	Utah	
Louisiana	West Virginia	
Maine	Wyoming	

Intermediate Departments (fifty to ninety-nine supervisors, field and institutional parole officers)

Alabama	Oklahoma	(8)
Colorado	Oregon	
Indiana	Tennessee	
Kentucky	Texas	

Large Departments (over one hundred supervisors, field and institutional parole officers)

California	New York	(14)
Florida	Ohio	
Georgia	Pennsylvania	
Michigan	South Carolina	
Minnesota	Virginia	
Missouri	Washington	
New Jersey	Wisconsin	

Appendix B

New York State Division of Parole Rules and Regulations

PROGRAM FOR PROFESSIONALIZATION OF STAFF

To enable the Division of Parole to retain the type of individual best qualified to carry on the exacting task of rehabilitating paroled offenders, the Board of Parole has developed a broad and comprehensive plan to attain this objective. This plan, as conceived by the Board of Parole, includes:

1. Additional professional training for present staff; and,
2. The maintenance of a professional atmosphere which will attract and retain qualified Parole Officer candidates and employees.

The scholarship program of the Division of Parole was initiated in September 1960. Work-study programs were planned with accredited Schools of Social Work and agreements reached which included part-time study while carrying full work assignment; such study to be preferably after normal working hours. Under such plans, replacement of staff members in part-time training would not be necessary allowing increased staff participation in the part-time program. It should be noted that temporary part-time replacement of staff requires approximately two-thirds of all scholarship funds, and that an exclusive full-time school attendance program would severely limit the number of staff enrolled. There are presently three programs by which graduate study may be accomplished, namely, (1) evening courses, (2) part-time work-study programs, and (3) full-time school attendance. In order to attain the Master's degree in Social Work, at least one academic year must be spent in full-time attendance in some schools, two years in others.

Contracts providing for graduate training for staff members have been made with the graduate schools of social work at Columbia University, Fordham University, Adelphi University, State University at Albany, Syracuse University, and State University at Buffalo. Staff members are required to attend the school closest to the area or institutional office in which they are employed with the exceptions of the Rochester staff who may choose between the Syracuse and Buffalo schools, the Poughkeepsie staff who may choose between either of the New York City schools and the Albany school, and the New York staff who may choose between the Fordham and Columbia schools.

In order to maintain a scholarship quota fairly distributed between each area office, and between area and institutional offices, separate lists of applicants have been prepared for each office according to the staff member's choice of schools and his seniority. Seniority will be computed from the date of permanent appointment as a Parole Officer followed by continuous service. Any Parole Officer who resigns and who is reinstated or reappointed within one year thereafter shall be deemed to have continuous service.

Agreements have been reached whereby student field instruction units have been installed in our New York, Buffalo, Syracuse, and Albany Area Offices in which some of our enrolled staff members may complete one-half of their field work requirements. This achievement provides distinct advantages:

(a) Our staff may complete half their field work in a familiar environment.

(b) Our staff has the opportunity, as students, of correlating and consolidating the most advanced social work knowledge and techniques in the setting to which they will return to work.

Scholarship awards provide payment for tuition and fees, basic books required and temporary replacements, when necessary, and include educational leave of absence with pay. Transportation costs are not allowable or reimbursable. A Screening Board evaluates all scholarship applications. In awarding scholarships, the following factors are given reasonable consideration:

1. Length of service in the Division of Parole.
2. Study completed in accredited schools at own expense prior to and during service with the Division of Parole.
3. Length of time necessary to complete work towards a degree.
4. Relative cost of the proposed educational program with respect to available funds.
5. Relationship to the agency's basic responsibility to first service the community, the parolees, and their families.

The scholarship program is designed to provide professional training in the field of social work. Scholarship awards will be made *only* to staff members for enrollment in courses in accredited graduate schools of social work in a program leading to the Master's degree in Social Work, Social Service or Social Welfare. Courses in related fields, under-graduate courses or doctoral study will not be considered eligible for scholarship awards, nor will any staff member who enrolls in a school of social work without requesting or receiving scholarship assistance, be granted such assistance until such time as he would normally have become eligible to begin studies under the Division's program.

In order to assure fair and equal treatment to all participants in this program, a contract similar to that used by all agencies in our field must be signed by all those receiving scholarships. The contract, as approved by the Attorney General's Office, states as follows:

STATE OF NEW YORK   EXECUTIVE DEPARTMENT
                                DIVISION OF PAROLE

STATE OF NEW YORK ⎤

COUNTY OF_____ ⎦

In consideration of my acceptance of a scholarship to participate in the program of recruitment and training of professional personnel of the Division of Parole in the Executive Department of the State of New York, I hereby waive the normal accumulation and liquidation of annual leave and sick leave credits and agree that during such participation such credits shall be accumulated and liquidated in accordance with the following schedule:

1. Persons in the program requiring them to be absent for one day or less per week will accumulate full leave accruals and may use them in the normal manner. (This is based on the assumption that such individuals will be carrying a normal work load.)

2. Persons involved in programs requiring them to be absent more than one day per week but less than full time will accumulate accrued leave time in proportion to the number of days that they work. Prior and current accruals will be utilized at the discretion of the supervisor.

3. Persons involved in full-time student programs will neither accumulate nor liquidate accrued leave time for the duration of their student program. In addition to the school holidays they will be entitled to one week's vacation following the termination of the academic year. Following their return to duty they will be entitled to use leave time accrued prior to their entering into the student program.

I further agree that upon completion of such scholarship training I shall remain employed by the Division of Parole unless my employment shall be terminated by suspension or dismissal from service in accordance with the Civil Service Law of the State of New York or by reason of my physical or mental disability, to continue in such employment for one calendar year for each full school year or equivalent of the training I shall have received under said program. Completion of 30 credit hours will be considered the equivalent of a full school year.

If it becomes necessary for me to leave employment of the Division of Parole by reason of physical or mental disability, I agree to furnish said Division with such medical evidence as it may require.

Should I fail to remain employed by the Division of Parole by reason of my suspension, dismissal from service or voluntary resignation on my part, I agree to reimburse the Division of Parole in the amount disbursed by the said Division covering all tuition and fees incurred by me in the course of my studies, within thirty (30) days of my termination as aforesaid.

Sworn to before me this

_____ day of _____, 19__

Notary Public

ACCEPTED BY:

Division of Parole

Scholarship applicants must designate the school of their choice, where more than one school is available, at the time of application. To avoid conflict and provide for an orderly administration of the separate school programs, the following procedures have been adopted:

1. Staff members must make a specific choice of one school and no one may be on more than one school list at any time.
2. Once a staff member begins a specific school program and enrolls for any course, he may not transfer to any other program.
3. Staff members enrolled in part-time courses will report to Director of their Area or Institutional Office at the end of each semester concerning the completion of the courses and the grade attained.
4. When a staff member in the scholarship program has previously earned credits acceptable to his chosen social work school within the agency program, the time of his participation in the full-time program may be accelerated to permit the student to take advantage of the earned credits within the 5 year limitation period.
5. When a staff member files an application for participation in the scholarship program he will be placed on the list below those already in the program, but in order of seniority with those who have not yet begun.
6. When a staff member is promoted to a supervisory level he will not supersede those staff members in a similar grade who are participating in the scholarship program on a part-time basis although he may have employee seniority over them. He will precede those who have not entered the program according to his seniority.
7. Staff members who are not accepted for full-time participation in the school of their selection, but are granted permission by the school to reapply at a later date, will be retained on the list of their original selection, but will go to the bottom of the list existent at the time of their rejection. They will have seniority over subsequent additions to the lists.

Staff members who have completed courses in the school of their choice and who are advised by the school that their performance has been unsatisfactory, or are dropped from their studies by the school for any reason, will not be permitted to apply to any other school and their scholarship award will be immediately terminated upon receipt of such notice from the school.

8. When a staff member is referred by the agency to a specific school to enroll for (1) a part-time course, (2) more than one part-time course, or (3) full-time enrollment, he will be considered to be actively involved in a school program and cannot be superseded by another staff member by reason of mere seniority on the staff. This presupposes, however, that he will remain of his own volition in continuous attendance at school on a full- or part-time basis until he complete his studies toward his M.S.W.

Interruption at the request of the school and/or the agency will not affect his status. However, interruption of studies of his own volition will be governed by the following action:

INTERRUPTION OF SCHOOL PROGRAM BY NON-ATTENDANCE AT CLASS OR FIELD WORK ASSIGNMENT

The principle that has been operative in this regard has been that a student who *"withdrew"* from the program, during its active phase, would be placed at the bottom of the list if he wished to resume his studies in the program.

While the principle was presumed to be clear and equitable, the many meanings implicit or permitted by the word *"withdrew"* were not anticipated. The present rule, therefore, categorizes the various meanings of *"withdrew"* and the consequences flowing from each category. They apply to both part-time and full-time students or applicants.

A. *Voluntary non-appearance at class or field work assignment.*

A student may voluntarily fail to appear at class or field work assignment for many reasons. A partial or non-exhaustive list of such reasons would include the following:

1. A desire to drop out of the school program as unsuitable for the student.
2. Lack of interest.
3. Excessive "cutting" of classes or field work.
4. Avoidance of examinations.
5. Non-completion of assignments.

A student in such a category might wish to change his mind at a later date. In that event he would have to submit a new application to the Division of Parole. If this application were accepted by the Division the applicant would be placed at the bottom of the then current list for his chosen school and would maintain this position for future consideration. Acceptance by the Division of such an ap-

plication would be discretionary on the part of the Division.
B. *Involuntary non-appearance at class or field work assignment.*
A student may have an earnest desire to continue in the scholarship program but be rendered unable to continue for reasons beyond his control and for which he is not culpable. These may include at least the following categories:

1. *Illness*—Incapacitating regarding class room and/or field work attendance.

Illness, in and of itself, is not scholastically incapacitating. It becomes scholastically incapacitating if the absence from the program is to a degree that precludes the granting of credit by the school.

A student forced to interrupt his school program because of illness, incapacitating to the degree of non-credit, will resume his place in the program at the earliest opportunity if he has not been replaced in the program by the following semester by the next student in line. If he has been replaced, he will be placed at the top of the appropriate waiting list.

2. *Accident and/or injury.*
   a. *service connected*—incapacitating regarding classroom and/or field work attendance.
   b. *non-service connected*—incapacitating regarding classroom and/or field work attendance.
   In the event of an accident with resultant injury or an injury not the result of an accident (assault, etc.) the same rules will apply as in the case of an illness, if the absence results in the non-granting of credits by the school.

In any event, any interruption of studies must be reported to the student's area or institutional Director or Supervisor in writing with advice concerning the student's desire to permanently terminate his school program, or re-enter the program at such time as he is eligible for reconsideration.

9. Staff members attending school on a part-time basis who are offered the opportunity to apply for full-time attendance and request postponement, or for any reason other than personal illness or accident do not make such application, will be placed on the appropriate list below those already attending on a part-time basis but before those who have not yet started any school courses.

While it is desirable to retain as much flexibility as possible in administration of the scholarship program, some controls are necessary to insure efficient operation. Basically, this program is one which has been established to improve our agency's ability to achieve its objectives by improving the level of our staff's professional ability. Therefore, the program is agency oriented and must be administered on the basis of that which is best for the Division of Parole. *Participation in the Scholarship Program must be considered a privilege and not a basic employee right superseding agency service to the public.*

The aforementioned rules and regulations will supersede those previously issued and are effective with the date of issue. They will not be retroactive nor will they effect any change of status of those staff members presently participating in the program or who have been referred to a school of social work for enrollment.

Appendix C

1969 Inventory of Personnel Practices in Adult Parole Systems

THE PENNSYLVANIA STATE UNIVERSITY
COLLEGE OF HUMAN DEVELOPMENT
CENTER FOR LAW ENFORCEMENT AND CORRECTIONS
(Please address replies to: Professor Charles L. Newman)

Part 1. Questions in this section are concerned with *recruitment* of prospective parole staff. Please indicate your usual practice even though your agency may not now be recruiting.

1.1 Who handles recruitment for parole staff?
____(a) Parole agency handles its own recruitment
____(b) State personnel agency (name_____)
____(c) Jointly between (a) & (b) above
____(d) Other (specify _____

1.2 What media are used for staff recruitment?
____(a) Announcements sent to a general mailing list
____(b) Newspaper announcements and advertising
____(c) Direct recruitment at college career days or with recruiters
____(d) Vacancies listed with the National Council on Crime and Delinquency (NCCD)
____(e) Vacancies listed with National Association of Social Workers (NASW)
____(f) Vacancies listed with American Correctional Association (ACA)
____(g) Requests made to other parole or probation agencies for nominations
____(h) Other (specify) _____

1.3 What is range of recruitment activities?
_____(a) Limited to state
_____(b) Limited to region
_____(c) National

1.4 Is recruitment limited to certain age groups?
_____(a) Yes
_____(b) No

1.5 What are range limitations?
_____(a) Men, minimum age
_____(b) Men, maximum age
_____(c) Women, minimum age
_____(d) Women, maximum age

1.6 On the reverse side of this page, or on attached sheet, please indicate any problems the parole agency has experienced in its recruitment activities.

Part II. Questions in this section are concerned with *selection* of prospective parole personnel. The aim is to determine current practices.

2.1 If your agency does *not* use a merit system or other form of competitive procedure for the selection of staff, please indicate in full detail how staff is selected.

2.2 When parole agency wishes to select new staff, which agency prepares examination?
_____(a) Parole agency
_____(b) State personnel agency
_____(c) Other (specify) _____

2.3 Are written examinations required?
_____(a) Yes   What agency administers examination?_____
_____(b) No   _____

2.4 Is a *rated* oral interview used?
_____(a) Yes
_____(b) No

2.5 Who participates in the oral interview of the applicant?
_____

2.6 How is previous experience of the applicant evaluated? Please describe briefly what factors are considered.

2.7 What are the educational requirements for the entry position as parole officer?

2.8 Is preliminary health examination required?
_____(a) Yes
_____(b) No

2.9 Is applicant required to provide references?
_____(a) Yes   _____personal; how many?_____
_____(b) No   _____experience; how many?_____
                 _____other; _____; how many_____

2.10 If references are required, how are they checked?
_____(a) By correspondence
_____(b) By personal investigation   (by whom)?_____
_____(c) Other_____

2.11 Are applicants for parole officer positions fingerprinted?
_____(a) Yes
_____(b) No

2.12 If so, are fingerprints cleared with Federal Bureau of Investigation?
_____(a) Yes   State Identification Bureau _____Yes
_____(b) No   _____No

2.13 Is previous *arrest* record a bar to employment?
_____(a) Yes
_____(b) No

2.14 Is previous felony *conviction* a bar to employment?
_____(a) Yes
_____(b) No

2.15 What are residence requirements at time of appointment?
_____(a) None
_____(b) One year (or less) in state
_____(c) Two years (or more than one) in state
_____(d) Residence rule may be waived. Please describe circum-
             stances.

2.16 Are veterans granted an employment preference?
_____(a) Yes
_____(b) No

2.17 If so, please describe policy with regard to this preference.

2.18 Are eligibility lists prepared for those candidates who have successfully
      passed examination?
_____(a) Yes
_____(b) No

2.19 If so, (2.18) please indicate procedure for appointment from eligibil-
      ity list. (For example: top man on list is appointed; state personnel
      provides choice of top three men, etc.)

2.20 Are staff appointed on a provisional or probationary basis prior to full
      appointment?
_____(a) Yes
_____(b) No

2.21 How long does probationary period last before parole officer is given
      a regular appointment?
_____(a) Six months or less
_____(b) Six months to one year
_____(c) Other (specify) _____

2.22 How many new field staff were appointed during 1967_____
                                        1968_____

2.23 How many positions for parole officers were budgeted but unfilled in 1968?_____

2.24 How many parole officers were separated from your agency during the probationary period *for cause* (that is, they were asked to leave) in 1967_____
1968_____

2.25 Does your agency permit "lateral entry" to supervisory-level positions?
_____(a) Yes
_____(b) No

PLEASE USE REVERSE SIDE OF THIS PAGE
FOR COMMENTS REGARDING ITEMS ON THIS PAGE.

2.26 Please describe relationship between parole agency and state personnel agency, if there is one in the state. Indicate also any problem areas experienced in the past several years regarding the appointment of staff. (Please continue on reverse of this sheet if more room is needed.)

Part III. Questions in this section are concerned with policy and practices related to *staff in-service training and development.* Please indicate *current* practice.

3.1 Does parole agency maintain a formal staff in-service training program?
_____(a) Yes
_____(b) No
_____(c) Plan to establish. When?_____

3.2 Please describe procedure for initial orientation for new staff members. (If orientation materials, manuals, etc., are available, may we have copies?)

3.3 Are funds budgeted specifically for staff training?
_____(a) Yes   How much per annum?_____
_____(b) No

3.4 Does parole agency have a full-time staff position which entails principal responsibility for the coordination of training functions?
_____(a) Yes   Title of position?_____
_____(b) No

3.5 Do *administrative* personnel have responsibility to conduct in-service training?
_____(a) Yes
_____(b) No

3.6 Do *supervisory* personnel have responsibility to conduct ongoing in-service training?
_____(a) Yes   How frequently?_____
_____(b) No

3.7   Who participates in the in-service training program?
_____(a) Limited to new staff members
_____(b) All field personnel
_____(c) All personnel, including supervisors, and administrators
_____(d) Other (specify) _____

3.8   Are *outside* consultants used for staff training purposes?
(Check all that apply.)
_____(a) University professors
_____(b) Personnel from other agencies such as the state personnel
        unit
_____(c) Correctional institution personnel
_____(d) Law enforcement personnel
_____(e) Other (specify) _____

3.9   Are parole staff *rated* as to *efficiency* of performance on the job?
_____(a) Yes   (Please provide sample of rating form.)
_____(b) No

3.10   How frequently are such service ratings made?
_____(a) Quarterly
_____(b) Semi-annually
_____(c) Annually
_____(d) Other (specify) _____

3.11   By whom is efficiency performance rating made?
_____(a) Immediate supervisor of employee
_____(b) Area of regional supervisor
_____(c) Administrative official
_____(d) Other (specify) _____

3.12   Is *final* efficiency rating discussed with individual employee?
_____(a) Yes
_____(b) No

3.13   What procedure is followed if efficiency rating of employee is less
       than satisfactory?

3.14   If parole agency does not use a *rating system* for staff evaluation,
       please describe manner in which staff efficiency, as well as "growth"
       and "development," are determined.

3.15   Does parole agency maintain a "work-study" or "trainee" program in
       conjunction with a college or university?
_____(a) Yes   Where?_____
_____(b) No   (Please attach details of Program)
_____(c) Planned; When?_____

3.16   What is parole agency policy and practice regarding staff leaves of
       absence for educational purposes? (Check all that apply.)
_____(a) Full salary
_____(b) Partial salary
_____(c) Full tuition
_____(d) Partial tuition
_____(e) No assistance, either salary or tuition.

3.17 Are field staff permitted to attend state, regional, or national professional meetings at agency expense? Please indicate policy and practice in this regard. (Check all that apply.)

_____(a) State meetings only

_____(b) Regional meetings only

_____(c) National meetings only

_____(d) Full expenses paid

_____(e) Partial subsidy

_____(f) No subsidy

_____(g) Participation limited to supervisors or executives

_____(h) Varies from year to year depending upon budget and location of meetings

3.18 Does parole agency have funds available for scholarships or other stipends for staff to allow for graduate training?

_____(a) Yes   (Please attach details, including source of funds.)

_____(b) No

3.19 If the response to 3.18 is *no*, has agency attempted to secure such funds?

_____(a) Yes   From whom?_____

         When:_____

_____(b) No

3.20 Does parole agency maintain a professional circulating library available to field staff, or similar collections in district or regional offices?

_____(a) Yes

_____(b) No

3.21 Please indicate any problems parole agency has experienced regarding staff training and development.

Part IV. Questions in this section are concerned with *compensation and career service* plans. Please attach salary schedules if available.

4.1 Are staff members of parole agency covered under a state civil service or merit system plan?

_____(a) Yes   Name of system_____

_____(b) No

4.2 Does parole agency maintain a range of salaries within a particular grade?

_____(a) Yes

_____(b) No

4.3 Are salary increases automatic within grade or based on merit?

_____(a) Automatic pay increases

_____(b) Based on merit. Please describe conditions for such an increase in salary.

4.4 Are employees granted vacation with pay?

_____(a) Administrative personnel; number of days per year _____

_____(b) Supervisory personnel: number of days per year _____

_____(c) Field personnel; number of days per year _____

4.5   What is policy regarding sick leave, with pay?
_____(a) Administrative personnel; number of days per year _____
_____(b) Supervisory personnel; number of days per year _____
_____(c) Field personnel; number of days per year _____

4.6   Please describe agency policy regarding disability incurred *in line of duty*.

4.7   Does parole agency maintain or participate in a retirement plan for staff? Please describe general provisions.

4.8   Where transportation is necessary for performance of job, what is agency policy?
(a) Employee operates own car
monthly allowance_____
mileage allowance _____
(b) Use of state vehicle_____
(c) Other _____

4.9   What is agency policy regarding *per diem* allowances?

4.10 What is agency policy in regard to overtime work?
Administrative personnel: _____(a) Compensatory time off
_____(b) Overtime pay
_____(c) No provision
Any limits?_____
Supervisory personnel: _____(d) Compensatory time off
_____(e) Overtime pay
_____(f) No provision
Any limits?_____
Field personnel: _____(g) Compensatory time off
_____(h) Overtime pay
_____(i) No provision
Any limits?_____

4.11 What is agency policy regarding promotional positions?
_____(c) All positions are open-competitive *with* a residence requirements.
_____(b) All positions are promotional within the agency, and *not open* to outside competition.
_____(c) All positions are open-competitive *with* a residence requirement.

4.12 What is policy regarding administrative positions?
_____(a) Promotional
_____(b) Appointive   By whom?_____

4.13 Is parole agency permitted to make appointments at a salary above the minimum in the scale for grade?
_____(a) Yes
_____(b) No

4.14 Please indicate any problems which the parole agency has experienced regarding compensation of staff, career plans, promotional opportunity, or staff turnover.

Part V. Questions in this section are concerned with administrative organization regarding personnel.

5.1   Name of person completing this form:_____
      Title: _____
5.2   Name of agency:_____
5.3   If parole agency is a division of a larger department, please indicate name of parent unit: _____
      _____
5.4   Number of administrative personnel in parole agency:_____
5.5   Number of supervisory personnel in parole agency:_____
5.6   Number of field employees in parole agency:_____
5.7   Number of institutional parole officers under agency control:_____
5.8   How many staff vacancies did parole agency have as of July 1, 1969?
      _____(a) Administrative
      _____(b) Supervisory
      _____(c) Field
5.9   In order to assure administrative and operating efficiency, how many additional positions are now needed in order to achieve agency's mission?
      _____(a) Administrative
      _____(b) Supervisory
      _____(c) Field
5.10 Please indicate the volume of staff turnover during:
      1967 (a)_____
      1968 (b)_____
5.11 What are the major reasons for staff turnover?
5.12 Comments:

Bibliography

American Assembly: *The 48 States: Their Tasks As Policy Makers and Administrators.* New York, Columbia University Press, 1955.

American Correctional Association: *Director of Correctional Institutions and Agencies of the U.S.A., Canada and Great Britain.* Washington, The American Correctional Association, 1968.

American Correctional Association: *Manual of Correctional Standards.* Washington, The American Correctional Association, 1966.

Anderson, Howard J., (Ed.): *Public Employee Organization and Bargaining.* Washington, Bureau of National Affairs, Inc., 1968.

Anshen, Melvin: Executive development — in-company vs. university programs. *Harvard Business Review, 32*: September, 1954.

Belcher, David W.: *Wage and Salary Administration.* Englewood Cliffs, N.J., Prentice-Hall, 1959.

Benjamin, Judith G., Freedman, Marcie K., and Lynton, Edith F.: *New Role for Nonprofessionals in Corrections: Pros and Cons.* Washington, U.S. Department of Health, Education and Welfare, 1966.

California Department of Corrections: *A Report to the Legislature on the Work Unit Parole Program.* Sacramento, Calif., California Department of Corrections, 1968.

Case, Harry L.: *Personnel Policy in a Public Agency.* New York, Harper, 1955.

Civil Service Assembly of the United States and Canada: *Employee Training in the Public Service.* Chicago, The Assembly, 1941.

Civil Service Assembly of the United States and Canada: *Placement and Probation in the Public Service.* Chicago, The Assembly, 1946.

Civil Service Assembly of the United States and Canada: *Oral Tests in Public Personnel Selection.* Chicago, The Assembly, 1942.

Civil Service Assembly of the United States and Canada: *Recruiting Applicants for the Public Service.* Chicago, The Assembly, 1942.

Cleveland, Frederick A., and Buck, A. S.: *The Budget and Responsible Government.* New York, Macmillan, 1920.

Conrad, John: *Crime and Its Correction: An International Survey of Attitudes and Practices.* Berkeley, Calif., University of California Press, 1965.

Corson, John J.: *Executives for the Federal Service.* New York, Columbia University Press, 1952.

Council of State Governments: *Reorganizing State Government.* Chicago, The Council of State Governments, 1950.

Cunniff, John: Employment tests deprive business of good workers. *Reporter Dispatch, 52*: March 25, 1968.

Diamond, Harry: Factors in planning and Evaluating in-service training programs. *Journal of Criminal Law, Criminology, and Police Science, 53*(4): 1962.

Etzioni, Amitai: *A Comparative Analysis of Complex Organizations.* New York, Free Press of Glencoe, 1961.

Etzioni, Amitai: *Modern Organizations.* Englewood Cliffs, N.J., Prentice-Hall, 1966.

Finer, Herman: *Administration and the Nursing Services.* New York, Macmillan, 1957.

Follett, Mary: *The Illusion of Final Authority.* A Paper presented at the meeting of the "Taylor Society." New York, December, 1926. (Reproduced by the Bureau of Employment Security, Federal Security Agency, March 1941.

Gaus, John M.: The theory of organization in public administration. *The Frontiers of Public Administration.* Berkeley, Calif., University of California Press, 1936.

Glaser, Daniel: *The Effectiveness of A Prison and Parole System.* Indianapolis, Bobbs-Merrill, 1964.

Gulik, Luther: Science, Values, and Public Administration. In Donald C. Rowatt (Ed.): *Basic Issues in Public Administration.* New York, Macmillan, 1965.

Harmon, Maurice A.: Unravelling administrative organization in state juvenile services. *Crime and Delinquency, 13*: July, 1967.

Heyns, Garrett: Patterns of correction. *Crime and Delinquency, 13*: July, 1967.

Ives, Jane K.: Basic training for probation officers. *Social Work, 8*: July, 1963.

Johnson, Elmer H.: *Crime, Correction, and Society,* rev. ed. Homewood, Ill., Dorsey Press, 1968.

Joint Commission on Correctional Manpower and Training: *Criminology and Corrections Programs: A Study of the Issues.* Washington, 1968.

Joint Commission on Correctional Manpower and Training: *Targets for In-Service Training.* Washington, The Commission, 1967.

Jucius, Michael J.: *Personnel Management,* 6th ed. Homewood, Ill., Richard D. Irwin, 1967.

Katz, Daniel: Human interrelationships and organizational behavior. In Sidney Mailick and Edward H. Van Ness (Eds.): *Concepts and Issues in Administrative Behavior.* Englewood Cliffs, N.J., Prentice-Hall, 1962.

Klein, Alice C.: *Civil Service in Public Welfare.* New York, Russell Sage Foundation, 1940.

MacKinnon, Donald W.: The Identification and Development of Creative Personnel. *Personnel Administration,* 31(1):1968.

Mailick, Sidney, and Van Ness, Edward H., (Eds.): *Concepts and Issues in Administrative Behavior.* Englewood Cliffs, N.J., Prentice-Hall, 1962.

Mayers, Lewis: *The Federal Service, A Study of the System of Personnel Administration of the United States Government.* New York, Macmillan, 1922.

Merton, Robert: *Social Theory and Social Structure.* Glencoe, Free Press, 1949.

Meyers, Charles A.: Basic employment relations. In Arthur Kornhauser, Robert Dubin, and Arthur M. Ross (Eds.): *Industrial Conflict.* New York, McGraw-Hill, 1954.

Moore, Harold E., and Walters, Newell B.: *Personnel Administration in Education.* New York, Harper, 1955.

Morris, Albert, and Powers, Edwin: *The Role of New England Colleges and Universities in Correctional Staff Education. Report of the New England Correctional Manpower and Training Project.* Boston, Massachusetts Correctional Association, 1968.

Morse, N. C.: *Employee Satisfaction, Supervision, and Morale in an Office Situation.* Ann Arbor, University of Michigan Survey Research Center, 1953.

Mosher, William E., and Kingsley, J. Donald: *Public Personnel Administration,* rev. ed. New York, Harper, 1941.

National Council on Crime and Delinquency: *Correction in the United States: A Survey for the President's Commission on Law Enforcement and Administration of Justice.* New York, National Council on Crime and Delinquency, 1966.

National Parole Institutes: *A Survey of the Organization of Parole Systems.* New York, National Council on Crime and Delinquency, 1963.

National Probation and Parole Association: Report of the National Conference on Parole. *Parole in Principle and Practice.* New York, The Association, 1957.

Newman, Charles L.: *Sourcebook on Probation, Parole, and Pardons,* 3rd ed. Springfield, Ill., Thomas, 1970.

Newman, Charles L.: Educational issues and strategies for the field of corrections. *The Quarterly* (The Pennsylvania Association on Probation, Parole, and Corrections), *34*: Spring, 1967.

Newman, Charles L., and Vallance, Theodore: Higher education and state government: opportunities for cooperation in the administration of justice. *Attorney General's Bulletin (Pennsylvania), 3*(2): 1969.

Newman, Charles L., and Hunter, Dorothy Sue: Education for Careers in Law Enforcement: An Analysis of Student Output 1964-67. *Journal of Criminal Law, Criminology, and Police Science, 59*(1): 1968.

Nigro, Felix A.: *Public Administration Readings and Documents.* New York, Rinehart, 1951.

Office of Education, U.S. Department of Health, Education and Welfare: *Projections of Educational Statistics to 1975-76.* Washington, 1966.

Pennsylvania Council for Correctional Staff Development: *Education for Career Service in the Correctional Field.* University Park, Pa., The Council, 1963.

Pennsylvania Crime Commission: *Task Force Report.* Harrisburg, Pa., Office of the Attorney General, 1969.

Pfiffner, John M.: *The Supervision of Personnel,* 2nd ed. Englewood Cliffs, N.J., Prentice-Hall, 1958.

Piven, Herman, and Alcabes, Abraham: *The Crisis of Qualified Manpower for Criminal Justice: An Analytic Assessment with Guidelines for New Policy.* Washington, U.S. Department of Health, Education, and Welfare, 1969, Vol I-II.

Piven, Herman, and Alcabes, Abraham: *Education and Training for Criminal Justice: A Directory of Programs in Universities and Agencies 1965-67.* Washington, U.S. Department of Health, Education, and Welfare, 1968.

Piven, Herman, and Alcabes, Abraham: *Education, Training, and Manpower in Corrections and Law Enforcement.* Washington, U.S. Department of Health, Education, and Welfare, 1966. Sourcebooks I-IV.

Polk, Kenneth: *The University and Corrections: Potential for Collaborative Relationships.* Washington, Joint Commission on Correctional Manpower and Training, 1969.

President's Commission on Law Enforcement and the Administration of Justice: *Task Force Report: Corrections.* Washington, Government Printing Office, 1967.

Prigmore, Charles S., (Ed.): *Manpower and Training for Corrections: Proceedings of an Arden House Conference.* New York, Council on Social Work Education, 1966.

Shartle, Carroll L.: *Executive Performance and Leadership.* Englewood Cliffs, N.J., Prentice-Hall, 1956.

Tebow, Hilda P.: Staff Development as an Integral Part of Administration. Washington, Government Printing Office, 1959, Public Assistance Report No. 35.

Torpey, William G.: Promotion from within. *Public Personnel Review, 13*: October, 1952.

U.S. Attorney General: *Annual Report of the Attorney General of the United States,* 1939. Washington, Government Printing Office, 1939.

U.S. Children's Bureau: *Training Personnel for Work with Juvenile Delinquents.* Washington, Government Printing Office, 1954.

U.S. Department of Labor: *Manpower Development and Training in Correctional Programs.* Washington, Government Printing Office, 1968.

U.S. Department of Justice, Office of Law Enforcement Assistance: *Strategies for Meeting Correctional Training and Manpower Needs.* Washington, Government Printing Office, 1966.

Western Interstate Commission for Higher Education: *Undergraduate Education and Manpower Utilization in the Helping Services.* Boulder, Colo., The Commission, 1967.

INDEX

123